The Complete Deer Hunt

By Joe DeFalco

GROSSET & DUNLAP

A NATIONAL GENERAL COMPANY

PUBLISHERS • NEW YORK

CONTENTS

FOREWORD

Recently it has become increasingly obvious to me that a book incorporating all the basic information about deer hunting, safety, field-dressing of deer, proper care of the venison and even recipes would be invaluable to the veteran as well as the novice hunter. The idea took hold on October 21, 1968. I had agreed to give a lecture, demonstrating the proper way to field-dress a deer. The story had received only a brief mention in Frank Keating's Hunting column in *The Long Island Press* in New York, but when I arrived at my store, I was amazed to see hundreds of people gathered in front.

Within minutes after the doors were opened, the store was jammed with eager hunters. The police had to be called to unsnarl the traffic that had backed up for six blocks in all directions. The Police Department later estimated that two to three thousand hunters had had to be turned away because of inadequate facilities.

This story was also written up in the newspapers and, by the following Saturday, I had received over fifty-six hundred letters from hunters. Their questions ranged from "What kind of rifle should I buy?" to "Where can I get some good venison recipes?" I did my best to answer all the questions, but then realized that if I could put all this into a compact "take-along" book, *The Complete Deer Hunt,* hundreds of thousands of hunters across the country would be able to look up whatever they personally needed to know about hunting.

I hope I've succeeded in writing the kind of book that you want. But if, after reading it, you still have some questions about hunting, or venison or any part of this book, I will be glad to answer your questions by mail. Just write to me—Joe DeFalco, Box 37 Franklin Square, New York, New York 11010 (Please send a self-addressed, stamped envelope.)

Now, happy reading—and good hunting

Joe DeFalco

The Complete Deer Hunt

1. INTRODUCTION TO HUNTING

Hunting is one of the most popular sports in this nation of ours. Each year the number of hunters increases, the younger men becoming just as intensely enthusiastic about the sport as the veterans. Whether the hunters are sixteen or sixty, when the hunting season nears, the same excitement and sense of anticipation overwhelm them. For a true hunter, the season never ends. Although the season may be closed, the conversation among fellow hunters, the feeling for the sport, the review of past experiences and the planning for new trips continue year around.

1

In New York State in 1969, there were 575,000 licensed big game hunters. This was a definite increase over those registered in 1968. The trend has been on the rise for the past few years. More and more people are beginning to realize that hunting is a healthy and rewarding sport. Previously, it was judged by many to be either too dangerous or too cruel to be considered a sport. Now, however, these people are taking another look.

Some of the most prominent men in our history including presidents, have been fellow hunters. The walls of Teddy Roosevelt's home, now a museum, in Oyster Bay, Long Island, New York, sport numerous trophies which symbolize his world-wide success as a hunter. The vitality, the determination, and the strength of character that he demonstrated are qualities still to be admired, still to be striven for.

Hunting is a fine sport, a sport which can contribute greatly to the total development of our young men. As we all know, and as sad as it may be, there is a wider generation gap than ever before. Unless steps are taken now to help bridge that gap, the problem will become even more acute. One step would be for father and son to share the experience of hunting, competing at the same time on equal terms. Wives and mothers can not only share the sense of anticipation of the hunt but they too may actually participate. Each year there are more licensed women deer hunters in New York State. Hunting can be one of those rare family sports. In addition to bringing great personal pleasure and satisfaction, we can only hope that, with time, an interest in hunting could help in one way or another to foster understanding between the generations and serve as a base for wholesome family relationships.

For all who share the experience of hunting, the rewards are many. There is a feeling of well-being, a sense of freedom and a new burst of energy. The beauty of nature can be more fully appreciated when you have walked over mountain trails scuffing the autumn leaves or setting tracks in the freshly fallen snow. It is only then that you understand the universal appeal of that grand old sport of hunting.

Remington Model 660 Magnum bolt action rifle

Remington Model 760 pump action rifle

Remington Model 742 autoloading rifle

2. BUYING A RIFLE

As a prospective hunter, you should buy a rifle only after you have carefully considered its many features. It has been proven time and time again, that the new hunter will usually buy two rifles before he settles on one that really suits his needs. It is only after his initial experience with it in the field, that the hunter finds that the gun he has chosen is either dangerous, useless or inadequate. Choosing the correct rifle is most important. For the average hunter the 30-06 caliber is the most popular. This caliber rifle comes in different models, some of which are the bolt action, pump, lever and semi-automatic. Let us consider the various types one at a time. Although quite popular because of its price, the lever model has one particular cause for concern. The release of the hammer has to be done most cautiously. In my twenty five years experience in hunting I have seen two hunters killed by lever (hammer) type rifles which fired accidentally while the hunter was resetting the safety lock. In winter time, with the trigger finger chilled or numbed by the cold, the control becomes even more difficult. Even though thousands of hunters use this model successfully, I believe this rifle is not for the novice.

The bolt action gun is a good safe rifle. With a gun of this type, however, much depends on hitting your target with the first shot. If you miss, too much time is wasted rejecting the bullet, reloading and re-aiming. You may have lost your one opportunity to get your deer. The average bolt action rifle holds between five and seven rounds of ammunition. It is best to check the individual state regulations as to the maximum number of bullets that can be loaded into the magazine at one time. Many hunters are misled by the idea that because the United States Army has used the bolt-action type, this should be a superior type of gun. But there is a difference between Army warfare and deer hunting.

It is unfortunate and often times disappointing for some hunters to wait as long as three to four years before they get the opportunity to shoot at a deer. Therefore, the accuracy of your shot is just as important as your choice of gun.

The pump gun is a fine rifle but, like any other, it can be very deadly. It is considered the second fastest firing rifle, much faster than a bolt or lever action rifle. While firing a pump gun, you never have to take your eyes off the target. You do, however, "shake" a little more due to the constant movement of your arm and shoulder when firing than you do with a semi-automatic. The pump gun was considered one of the most popular guns until the semi-automatic became available. But thousands of hunters still use the pump gun and probably would never switch. This rifle, as well as the others mentioned, also comes in various calibers. Though all are good for deer hunting, the 30-06 has proven to be one of the most effective and frequently used.

As hunting becomes an even more popular sport, the use of the semi-automatic is becoming more widespread. Inasmuch as it is possible to shoot as many as five bullets in seconds without taking your eyes off the deer, you have a great advantage when using a semi-automatic. In the event you miss on your first shot, there is still time for a second and third one. Another advantage of the semi-automatic is that, if necessary, the magazines can be switched and the rifle reloaded very quickly. It can be heartbreaking for a hunter to stand there with an empty rifle while a big buck poses for what could have been a perfect shot. This rifle is light in weight, easy to handle and comes in various calibers. Extra magazines can easily be carried.

In some states and counties, only the shotgun is permitted for deer hunting. In the state of Pennsylvania the semi-automatic rifle is illegal, while in its neighbor state of New Jersey all rifles are illegal for deer hunting. In New Jersey, deer are killed with 00 buckshot and nothing else. On the other hand, the use of 00 buckshot on deer is illegal in New York State. This should give you an idea of the many conflicting laws in different states. Laws, however, are made to be followed and a smart hunter checks them all before he goes afield.

The shotgun is also a very effective gun. Some counties in New York allow only shotguns with rifle slugs and other counties allow both rifle and shotgun. The most popular shotgun, the twelve gauge, is often used for small-game as well as for deer. Again these guns come in categories. There are bolt action, single barrel, double barrel, pump and semi-automatic shotguns. The semi-automatic, here again, has proven to be the most popular.

Proper care of your gun is essential. Keep it clean and well oiled at all times. Your gun should be locked in a closet and out of the reach of children. Safety is one cardinal rule of hunting. It should be your first thought when your gun is at home, at the range or in the field. The same care and caution should be taken with your ammunition. The life you save may be your own or that of a loved one.

Now that you have chosen your gun, it is important that you familiarize yourself with it. A smart hunter goes to the range several times before the season begins. Shooting at a bull's eye and knowing you can hit it is an excellent practice, but when the deer season rolls around it is better to set up life-size deer targets. The biggest deer stands only thirty six inches from hoof to shoulder, so setting a target six feet in the air is practically useless. Target shooting is just a way of practice, so why practice on the drums if you plan to play the piano.

I've often been asked, "What is the most effective shot to down a deer?" Unfortunately, the hunter is often in a position where the most effective shot (into the vitals) will not be possible and he will have to do the best he can under the circumstances.

Theoretically, the most effective and telling shots would be into the neck, either cutting the spinal nerve and causing the deer to fall, or hitting the large artery or vein in the neck causing very heavy bleeding. A head shot, causing injury to the brain, is also a vital one; however, this also destroys the possibility of getting a good trophy. A shot through the shoulder, or angled behind it, or directly through the forward part of the chest may hit the heart. At times, even though the heart may be hit, the deer may continue to run a considerable distance before it falls. That is why I emphasize the value of the semi-automatic rifle which allows a quick (and merciful) following shot if necessary.

One of the biggest mistakes hunters make, the veteran as well as the novice, is to zero their rifles in on the range using a different grain of bullet than that which they plan to use on the hunt. The grain of the bullet, a measure of its weight, affects the velocity, distance and striking power of the bullet. At two hundred yards, a change in grain could cause a shift of six to twelve inches, maybe more, in the bullet's flight path by the time it reaches the target. A smart hunter will sight his gun at a target about one hundred yards distant, using the same grain of bullet he plans to use in the field.

The right ammunition for your rifle is as important as the gun itself. Some hunters use 130 grain bullets for deer hunting, although this grain is too light. You may find that 180 grain is more acceptable and that a 220 grain is far better. Then there will be no doubt in your mind, that if you hit your target deer, he will go down.

To get ready for the deer season, set up your targets, use the right grain of bullet and learn to fire your gun as fast as you can. Know your rifle like you know your job, or the car you drive. The more you practice with it, the better shot you will be; and the faster you learn to shoot it, the more chances you will have to down your deer. But remember, in most cases safety depends on you, regardless of where you are. And coming home safely to tell your family all about the hunt is going to be as much fun and excitement as shooting your deer.

In summary, I believe that the final selection of a rifle or shotgun is one of individual decision. To each his own. Some hunters like a heavy rifle and a heavy grain of bullet. Others, particularly if they happen to be experts on the rifle range, prefer a light bullet that *must* hit in a vital spot. The type of terrain to be hunted and the state you are hunting in will also play a role in the selection of the right gun for you. Choose wisely, and with proper care and handling your gun will last a long time.

Now that you have selected your rifle and purchased it, remember these points:

1. All states require hunting licenses before you go afield.

2. Licenses may have to be obtained separately for both big game and small game.

3. Some states have laws that make it compulsory that new hunters take a safety course. This course, usually of about four hours duration, is both interesting and helpful.

4. Some communities demand that firearms be registered. Check your local situation and comply with such regulations.

3.   THE LONGBOW

Our American Indian lived off the land, the bow and arrow his only weapon. Many a deer, buffalo and small-game animal were killed with the arrow. An arrow, like a bullet, has tremendous killing power when it hits in a vital area. Each year, archery is becoming a greater sport. Hunting with the longbow is a greater challenge because your method of hunting is more limited. There are certain advantages, however. Most states will allow either-sexed deer to be killed, and the season usually precedes the regular big game rifle season by a few weeks. In most states, a special license may be necessary, so check the local regulations.

As a prospective archer, you should buy a bow only after you have considered its many features. As with the hunter who purchases a rifle and finds that it does not suit his needs, so too it is not uncommon for a hunter to buy a bow that later proves unsatisfactory. But to buy a 75 pound bow a week before the season opens, then go afield only to find that you are having trouble stringing it or that you can only draw it half-way, is an example of unpreparedness. Problems like these can be avoided with just a little common sense. First, if you are just learning to shoot, you might try drawing one of your friend's bows just to get the feel of it. The average hunting-bow weight is between 40 to 65 pounds. When you are able to hold the bow at full draw for 20 to 30 seconds, you are capable of handling that particular weight. Naturally, you should begin practicing with a lower weight bow and work your way up.

A bow should be purchased long before the hunting season begins. You can build up your muscles easily, but it takes time. At least three weeks before you start to shoot arrows, use the bow to exercise with. Simply pull the string back, anchor, hold and bring your arm forward to the relaxed position again. When you are able to comfortably draw your bow to its full capacity, you can begin to practice with arrows. Remember, however, to provide a suitable back stop to your target, such as bales of hay, excelsior, straw, or a good target mat. Like the gun, the longbow is a deadly weapon. Arrows have been known to pierce flimsy targets and find unsuspecting victims behind. Also, until you are able to hit your target consistently, be sure that no one is loitering in and around the target area. Don't play William Tell! Your first shot may hit the dust three feet in front of your big toe, while your second may soar high over the target. Putting that arrow where you want it is a matter of time, practice and your knowledge of your bow.

Start shooting with practice arrows from a range of about twenty yards. Again, life-size paper deer targets set no higher than 36 inches from the ground are ideal. An 8-inch paper plate can be attached to the shoulder area of the target. Once you can hit the plate consistently, back up to forty yards and continue shooting. When you feel relaxed at this distance and can hit your target, move back to sixty yards. About two weeks before the deer season opens, begin practicing with your broadhead hunting arrows. Also, practice drawing your bow slowly. Often, when you are hunting, your target deer will be looking at you. If you draw

9

your bow with a sudden, fast motion, he will jump before you have the shot off. The time, from the start of the draw to the anchor should be about four seconds. While you are doing this, concentrate on picking out the spot on the deer you want to hit. When you are consistently able to hit your paper deer target at sixty yards using broadhead hunting arrows, you are ready to go afield.

4. YOUR HUNTING COMPANIONS

Your hunting companions are one of the most important factors in a happy, safe and successful hunt. Your life may depend on the people you are with, so choose them carefully. Most hunters are well-balanced, intelligent and safety conscious. On the other hand, there will always be that very small percentage who are definitely problems. Fortunately, many of these types can be determined ahead of time, and should be eliminated from your plans when forming your hunting group.

One of the best ways to meet sincere and efficient hunters and "regular guys" is to join a hunting club. There are thousands of them throughout the United States. Through your association with hunters on the firing range, on small-game hunts and through socializing with them, you will be given an opportunity to note their good and bad features. Safety must always be considered, as once again we state, your life depends on it. Hunting is a wonderful sport. Your hunting party determines how safe it is.

11

To discover on the first day of the deer season that some of your "buddies" do not want to get up in the morning is discouraging and could spoil the entire trip. Smart hunters are up at 5:00 A.M. and on the line at 6:00 A.M., wide awake and alert. Tired hunters are more apt to be careless, so a good night's sleep is imperative. If a friend wants to stay out all night and sleep till noon, leave him home!

One of the advantages of socializing with future hunting companions is to note how they act with others in a group and even how they handle alcohol. If someone in your group uses the hunting trip as just another excuse to drink, you may have to spend half a day sobering him up before sending him home. So why bring him in the first place? Alcohol and guns do not mix.

There are others who, with their chronic complaints, only aggravate the group and will prove to be undesirable. It is a basic part of the joy of the hunt that all the members of the group act together in a spirit of harmony and congeniality.

The novice hunter would make a wise decision to join with, work with and observe a veteran in action. As much as can be learned from reading, there is nothing like on-the-job training.

DeFalco and companions get ready for a successful hunt.

Perilous footing should be avoided, especially when carrying a loaded rifle. A stunt like this can ruin a hunt.

5. SAFETY AND PHYSICAL HEALTH

I cannot emphasize too much the need for safety from the time your rifle is purchased, while you have it stored at home, while you are cleaning or loading it, practicing with it, sighting it in, carrying it with you on the hunt and firing it. The lives of your loved ones, your friends and your own life are at stake, so be careful. The novice hunter has a responsibility to treat all matters pertaining to the hunt with interest and complete awareness of his responsibility, once a rifle is in his care. Free discussion of all problems involved with safety can and should be undertaken long before the hunt begins. You cannot be too safe.

A rifle is a deadly weapon and should always be treated as such. It should never be loaded in the house, or carried loaded in the car. While loading your rifle, concentrate on the job at hand. Step away from any group that you may be with—point the gun at the ground and put your safety on before you load. If the ground is extremely rocky, it is safer to angle the rifle skyward in order to avoid any accidental ricochet type shot.

13

At no time should a loaded or unloaded gun ever be pointed at a human being, even in jest. Too often we hear about the "unloaded" gun that fires and kills. And, as we have already stated, keep your weapon and ammunition locked up and out of the reach of children. Safety precautions and common sense should be used at all times. Be fair to yourself and to all the hunters who share the woods and fields with you. Carelessness is a serious defect—let it not be yours.

In fairness to all, the general health status of all members of your party should be good. The young, the middle-aged and the 'elders' may all love the sport; however, the physical problems of any member, heart trouble or a lung problem, with difficulty in breathing on heavy effort, must be made known to the other members. A diabetic, an epileptic, or an asthmatic should honestly bring forth his problem and consider seriously whether he should make the strenuous trip.

There are at least 575,000 registered deer hunters in New York State alone. Of them, you could expect that a certain percentage would have vision and/or hearing problems of some degree. Color blindness would also be present in a certain small percentage. The relative safety of your blaze-orange or red hunting clothing is of no use when one of your group (or any other hunter in your vicinity) is color blind. Color blindness, of course, cannot be corrected, but those defects that can be corrected, should be. False pride should not be allowed to stand in the way of using mechanical health aids (glasses, hearing aids, etc.) or using appropriate medication for chronic illnesses. Besides causing an unnecessary safety hazard, a man cannot fully enjoy even a successful hunt if he is not at the top of his form and as comfortable, under the strenuous hunting conditions, as it is possible for him to be.

Then there is the question of general body vigor. I would certainly urge those who plan a hunting trip to maintain the muscle tone and strength and health of their bodies all year round. It is foolhardy to get "soft" or over-weight for fifty weeks and then throw yourself into heavy physical effort for one day or two weeks. Keep yourself in shape with physical activities the year round. Perhaps, during one of your rare visits to your doctor, you could discuss such problems as weight, diet, smoking and the amount of extra activity that you can safely assume to toughen up your body, so that the vigor of the hunt can be easily tolerated.

Let us presume, now, you have downed your deer. Common sense and safety (depending on the size of the deer and the distance from your camp site) would determine whether you should attempt the difficult chore of dragging the deer to the camp by yourself. Ordinarily you should have help; so don't be ashamed to notify the other members of your party by walkie-talkie or prearranged signals. Don't try to be a hero. Don't let this be the time you get your first heart attack, by trying to "prove" yourself. It isn't necessary, and it is dangerous.

The manner in which you hunt can also be dangerous. The hunter who thinks that, by the use of camouflaged apparel and equipment, he is "hiding" from the deer is also "hiding" from his fellow hunters. A sudden move on his part may make him the target of an overanxious hunter.

In a similar way, a stand constructed eight to twelve feet high in a tree also creates a hazard. The hunter tends to be obscured by the foliage he may have in front of him and a stray shot could hit him. In the longbow season, a hunter perched high in a stand waiting for his deer may become the target of a small game hunter on the ground; for the longbow and small-game season quite often overlap. Think carefully before using camouflage and the stand. I personally consider them dangerous and never use either.

It is of basic importance that you leave your home and return to it safely. The dangers of the hunt should be foreseen and avoided. The physical demands of the sport should be anticipated and the body trained to easily tolerate them. Hunting is a great sport which can bring immense personal satisfaction, if it is approached with enthusiasm and attention to detail.

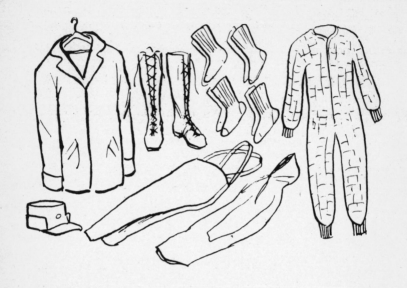

6. WEARING APPAREL

Selecting proper hunting gear is just as important as selecting the proper rifle. As we have determined previously that members of your group are safety conscious, we must consider that there are other groups in the woods with us. By wearing the right colors, movement and form can be more easily detected. It is now a law in many states that blaze-orange must be worn, since it has been proven that it can be seen at the greatest distance. Knowing your target is one thing but being aware that there may actually be someone behind the target is of greater importance. While hunting, you must always be aware of the presence of others, just as you expect them to be aware of your presence. The wearing of the proper clothing insures your safety as well as theirs.

For many years, bright red has been the most popular color. This color, as well as yellow, will still be seen in the years to come, and one is as good as the other. But blaze-orange has proven to be the most visible and therefore the safest. So, if you have not as yet purchased your apparel, or are buying new apparel,

16

you would be wise to adopt blaze-orange as the color of the future. (All state laws may eventually demand it.)

If the veteran has all his hunting clothes, a new outfit is not necessary. A blaze-orange vest, which costs only two or three dollars may be worn over the outer jacket or a blaze-orange cap may be obtained. As far as the color of hunting pants is concerned, yellow, bright red or blaze-orange should be satisfactory. The color of your shirt also has to be a safe one. Many times you will have to take off your outer jacket, so a blaze-orange shirt is absolutely necessary. A colorful handkerchief is also necessary for a white one, at a distance, can be mistaken for a white-tailed deer.

A smart hunter gets used to his clothes and his hunting boots long before the hunting season rolls around. Hunting clothes are warm and outdoor workers may be able to wear them even on the job. It is better to break in your hunting boots before the hunt, rather than on the first day. Walking is difficult enough, without blisters adding to your problems.

While the selection of the type of clothing may be difficult in areas of varying temperatures, the need for safe colors will always be present. The color of your clothes protects you. You have the responsibility to yourself and to your family to be dressed as safely as possible.

Following is a list of clothing needs for a three to four day hunting period. We must be aware that we may face clear and cold, snowy or rainy weather. Frequent changes may be necessary and proper gear must be available.

Suggested items:
1. Cap—with ear muffs.
2. Hunting jacket—two if possible.
3. Hunting pants—two if possible.
4. Hunting shirts—two.
5. Red thermal underwear—two sets.
6. Thermal socks—four pairs.
7. Thermal hunting boots.
8. Suspenders.
9. Rain gear—in bright color.

As far as suspenders are concerned, I would like to make one comment. I have personally found them to be comfortable to wear and efficient in holding the extra weight that may be carried in the large pants pockets, although I still wear a loose belt to support my knife. A tight belt and tight clothing limit freedom of movement and over a period of time can cause great discomfort. Safe clothing is always important, but why not be comfortable, too.

Joe DeFalco leads hunters toward the drive area. Note man on right is wearing a blaze-orange jacket which stands out better than various color reds.

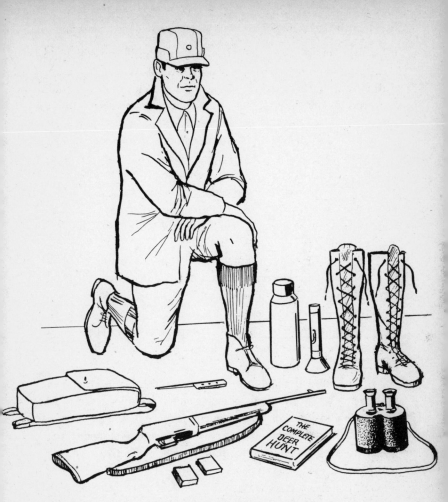

7. HUNTING EQUIPMENT

The type of equipment needed depends on the region where you are going to hunt. The following items are standard equipment, no matter where you hunt. The basic equipment would be the rifle, ammunition, knife, rope, blaze-orange cloth, compass, waterproof matches, disposable gloves and plastic bag for heart, liver and kidneys.

The walkie-talkie, while not vital, is a most helpful piece of equipment. A good set has a range of from three to five miles and can save hours of time and miles of walking. It helps the hunt become more effective because you can easily keep in touch with other members of your party. It also eliminates the possibility of members of the hunting party getting lost. Naturally, the more walkie-talkies there are in the group, the closer the contact among all its members. It is a great feeling to know ahead of time that a good sized buck is headed in your direction. You have time to release your safety, adjust your position and prepare for that vital shot. If by any chance you miss, you in turn, have the opportunity to alert the others. The walkie-talkie is light in weight and can be easily carried in any pocket. During the hunt the walkie-talkie is always carried in the "ON" position, and even when in your pocket, the reception is good. Only the voices of the hunters will be heard.

If you are camping out, other needed pieces of equipment will be a portable tent, sleeping bag, small stove, flashlight, first-aid kit, and hand-hatchet. In addition, you will need food supplies, including the canned variety. At least one day ahead of time, the camp site should be selected and completely set up. This saves time and allows you to be ready at sun-up for the first day of the hunt.

The sleeping bag is an important accessory. A new type, now on the market, features an amazing new "pop-out" zipper, to guarantee a fast exit in case of an emergency. It weighs only six pounds and can be used both summer and winter. Its inner lining weighs four pounds and, when in use, will be effective even to a temperature low of forty degrees below zero. In the warmer months, this lining is removed.

A well designed knife makes the job of field-dressing a deer properly a lot easier. Many hunters make the mistake of buying a 'pretty,' stainless steel knife, which is almost worthless, or a twenty dollar one which is only good for show. I recommend a Dexter boning knife which sells for about four dollars.

Some hunters have been found to be allergic to the deer's skin as they may be to dog or cat hair. The new disposable type of plastic glove, besides helping to eliminate this problem, also makes the task of field dressing a cleaner one. A large polyethylene type bag is used temporarily to store the gloves. After the deer is "dressed," the gloves are thrown away and the bag is used to carry the liver, heart and kidneys. The packaged combination

20

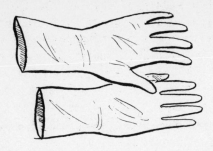

of gloves and bag sells for about one dollar and has proven most satisfactory.

A good tent shields you from the elements and makes your stay a pleasant one. In colder temperatures a space heater can be used to warm the chilled air.

The red or blaze-orange cloth we have mentioned is draped over the rack, partly over the deer, or close by as the deer is being "gutted," thereby eliminating the possibility that the downed deer might be mistaken for a bedded-down deer. The cloth should also be draped over the deer and tied securely before the deer is dragged or carried back to the camp site.

In summary, the type of equipment needed and the apparel that should be worn on the hunt depends on many factors; the area or type of ground that is to be hunted, the weather—rain or snow—and the temperature changes to be expected. Serious considerations should also be given to such matters as the length of stay in the hunting preserve, the type of sleeping and eating arrangements, the number of members in the hunting party, the degree of ruggedness of its various individuals, the distance from "civilized" communities and what last minute purchases can be made or services obtained near or at the hunting site. These and other variables, plus the use of common sense, will determine just what should be taken on the hunting trip to make it a successful, safe and enjoyable experience. I cannot possibly cover here all the situations of climate and terrain that you would need to make the final determinations. In many cases, therefore, the decisions and the experience of the veteran hunter in the local area should be the controlling and guiding influence.

CHECK LIST

Hunting Equipment

Rifle	——
Sling (for rifle)	——
Walkie-talkie	——
Disposable gloves	——
Dri-wipes	——
Hand warmer	——
Rain gear	——
Tent	——
Cot	——
Axes	——
Flashlight	——
Space heater	——
Extra batteries	——
Can opener	——
Waterproof matches	——
Map of area	——
Plastic bucket	——
Fountain pen	——
Roof rack (for car)	——
Cap (red or orange)	——
Underwear (red or orange)	——
Suspenders	——
Boots	——
Handkerchief (red)	——
Ammunition	——
Red or blaze-orange cloth (to cover deer)	——
Knife	——
Polyethylene bag	——
Compass	——
Sash cord	——
Sleeping bag	——

Air mattress	——
Tarpaulin	——
Saws	——
Sun glasses	——
Binoculars	——
First-aid kit	——
One burner stove	——
Cigarette lighter	——
Hand hatchet	——
Can of white spray paint	——
Back pack	——
Camera	——
Jacket (red or blaze-orange)	——
Socks (3-4 pair)	——
Belt	——
Laces (extra)	——
'Hot' pillows	——
Battery-heated socks	——

Food supplies

Sandwiches	——
Thermos (hot drink)	——
Canned soda	——
Salt	——
Chocolate bars	——
Canned fruit juices	——
Bottle of brandy	——

Check Car

Oil	——
Brakes	——
Gas	——
Air in spare tire	——

8.   THE HUNTING SITE

The novice, as well as the veteran, can save much time and effort by going directly to the county where the largest "kill" was recorded the previous year. This fact alone proves that there will be plenty of deer in the area. A review of the statistics released by the various state conservation departments will give excellent leads to new and perhaps profitable grounds.

A successful hunt demands a thorough knowledge of the area. Quite often the small game season precedes the big game season by a few weeks. Good hunters take advantage of this time to get to know the area. While pheasant or rabbit hunting, they can observe deer paths, areas where the deer are bedded down and

what they are eating. Apples, flowering dogwood and red maple are some of the "foods" that deer seem to favor. If this type of browsing foliage is not in evidence, if the trails are not seen and there is no sign of deer droppings, this is probably a poor area to hunt. On the other hand, many deer trails with droppings, good foliage and live beds, plus seeing the deer themselves, would be confirming evidence that this would be a good site for hunting in the near future.

It is always a good policy to get advance permission from the owner of the property on which you wish to hunt, if sufficient state land is not available. If the area is not "posted" you may legally hunt in that region. However, if the owner personally requests that you do not hunt his land, you should withdraw. When exploring a new area for the first time, you should always study a regional map to become familiar with the terrain.

Whenever I face a particularly heavily wooded area for the first time, I use what I think is quite an original method, a small can of white spray paint with which I mark a "trail." As I start into the woods, I spray a white streak across a tree trunk at about eye-level. Then, as I walk along through the woods, I mark other trees the same way, every fifty to seventy five feet depending on the density of the trees in the area. This "marking" should be done prior to opening day. The paint will stay on the trees for as long as one year, eliminating your chances of getting lost and saving you a lot of time in relocating that likely looking or favorite spot. Time is very important when hunting, and much time can be wasted wandering through the woods looking for a suitable spot. The hunting site should be selected in advance and, if possible, surveyed and marked.

There are many advantages to membership in a hunting club, one of which is that the majority of hunting clubs own their own land and have permission to "post" other land in the area. Local sports columns are sometimes very helpful in suggesting new regions in which to hunt. Veteran hunters can also inform you of areas where the deer are plentiful. Once you have full knowledge of the areas, your selection of a site should be agreed upon by all members of the party. Remember, harmony among the group helps to make your trip more enjoyable.

9. PLANNING AND MANAGEMENT

By now, you realize that planning and management are the keys to both a successful and enjoyable deer hunt. The rifles are ready and the hunters are trained in techniques. The hunting licenses have been checked. The equipment has been purchased and is in good condition. The hunting site has been chosen and even a "dry run" of the hunt may have been accomplished. Now the final steps of the preparation have to be taken. Reservations for the hotel or motel rooms should be made weeks in advance. If outdoor living is going to be the order of the day, food supplies, tent,

Each hunter must know the area and his assignment. A last-minute check to be sure.

sleeping bags, back packs, and other bulky equipment must be transported into the woods. Eating facilities at motels, diners, etc. should be checked out. Each hunting trip will have its own specific problems and the leader of the group—a veteran—should anticipate these problems and answer them one at a time. He must decide how many cars will be necessary, and the best route to be followed. When it is determined which cars and drivers will be utilized, congenial groups should be arranged for each vehicle.

The possibility of mechanical breakdown should be anticipated and an auxiliary plan discussed. Depending on the type of cooking and storage facilities available, the group leader must determine how much and what kinds of foods will be obtained and carried on the trip. The title of "cook first class" can now be bestowed on the most suitable subject. As far as sleeping arrangements are concerned, men that have similar interests, such as four or five card players, may ask to room together.

Upon arriving at the town nearest the hunting site, it is wise to check such routine but important items as the closing time of the gas station and stores, including the local drug store. Medical facilities should be quickly evaluated, telephone service checked out, and at least one call made by one member of the hunt to his wife to let her know of the safe arrival of the group.

Plans should be made to see that the individual hunter is warm, well-fed and kept as comfortable as possible. Hot drinks, sandwiches, candy and fruit may be carried by the hunters into the field if so desired. Between drives, the hunters may replenish their supplies from one of the cars which may be used as a temporary base of operation.

In planning the trip, it is a good idea to review the state regulations regarding hunting, paying particular attention to new laws. Cooperation with state authorities and landowners is important. Hunters should demonstrate courtesy at all times and express appreciation to the individual landowner for the privilege of hunting on his land. We can show this appreciation by respecting his property rights and keeping the area clean at all times. At the end of the hunt, a few of the hunters should thank him personally. Later on, the members can send individual notes of thanks. It is also a kind personal gesture to send a greeting card along during certain holiday seasons. Care and attention to all details—no matter how small—make the trip a pleasant human experience even if it unfortunately happens that you do not get your deer this time.

(I would like to make a special note at this point, of the appreciation that this author has for the efforts of the various state conservation departments. Every day, winter and summer, the deer population is kept under surveillance. The number, sex and age of the deer are estimated. The diseases and nutritional problems of the deer are evaluated and browsing areas are improved. With their recommendations, bulletins and magazines, the departments keep the individual hunter posted on the deer situation, in order that he may enjoy a good "harvest" of deer during the hunting season. I particularly want to thank the New York State Department of Conservation for the marvelous job it has done in the past and continues to do.)

Tag your deer immediately.

10. METHODS OF HUNTING

There are many different ways to hunt, and much depends on the terrain; whether it is flat, hilly, swampy or mountainous. Through necessity, my suggestions in this area are mainly for hunting the white-tail deer in the northeastern section of the country (mountainous with heavy brush and thickly wooded areas). Hunting conditions, naturally, change from state to state and specific hunting advice should be obtained from a veteran hunter in your area. In some states, for example, it may be necessary to use jeeps, snow-mobiles, sleds or horses to get to the hunting area. But, in New York State, it is illegal to shoot a deer from an automobile. So check the state's hunting regulations before you shoot, *and* before you decide to use certain methods of hunting. One method, for example, using dogs to run deer, is illegal in some states.

Other factors involved in what method of hunting you should use would be the number of hunters in your party and the time of day. The most frequently used techniques are stalking, sitting and driving.

29

STALKING

If you are hunting with just two or three companions, you might use the stalking method. Spread out about two hundred yards apart and begin walking forward very slowly, stopping every forty feet or so to look around. After a few moments, continue walking forward and repeat the procedure. This hunting method can also be used when you are hunting alone. In this type of hunting your rifle should be 'ready' at all times. Those who have heart trouble, get out of breath easily or are older, will find that this is an easy way to hunt, because there is no pressure involved and you can set your own pace. In this way, several miles can be covered in rather leisurely fashion. A circular course is sometimes of help because one can cover new terrain, while still returning to your original starting point. In stalking deer, it is absolutely essential to be as quiet as possible as you slowly advance.

In the event you shoot your deer, your buddies should be within shouting distance. As you walk along you may notice that some deer follow such confused courses that they will often come directly at you. You may also, occasionally, arouse a deer from its "bed." When a deer springs up in front of you and runs away, your shot may be of the more difficult variety. Seven out of ten

times, you only have its rump as a target. Don't hesitate in your shot! If you hit that deer, the deer almost always falls but be ready for a second shot. This method is still frequently used by the "loner" or when the group is very small. And it has proven extremely successful through the years.

SITTING

It is commonly known among the veteran that certain hunters have favorite "posting" spots from which to hunt. Because they have killed deer in the same location for several consecutive years some fellows feel that this is their lucky spot, and they will not desert it. This method of hunting requires a great deal of patience as days might pass before a deer is seen and a small folding chair certainly comes in handy. I've often observed hunters sitting on rocks, or leaning against trees waiting to spot a deer. As one old-time guide told me, "When you go hunting, you are never alone."

Sitting is excellent for fellows who are getting on in years or who prefer to take it easy while hunting. And, truthfully, a big percentage of deer are killed by "sitters." While it is quite safe to sit high on a rock, I do not recommend tree stands. They can be dangerous, since foliage may hide you from view and make you the target of an overanxious or careless hunter. In many states, trees are considered unsporting and have consequently been out-lawed. Therefore, it is advisable to check your state regulations before building a tree stand.

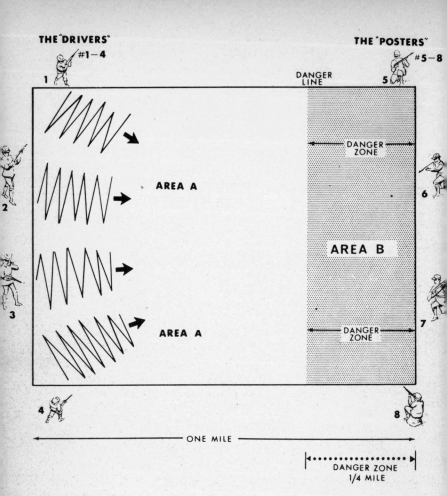

DANGER LINE

1

5

AREA A

DANGER ZONE

AREA B

2

6

3

AREA A

DANGER ZONE

7

4

8

ONE MILE

DANGER ZONE
1/4 MILE

11. THE DRIVE

The schematic above shows the technical elements of the drive, but it cannot convey in any way the excitement and the action of the drive. There are more deer killed on drives than with any other hunting method. In general, at least eight hunters should be used, but there are certain advantages if an even greater number take part. (Some states have laws that limit the size of these groups and such regulations should be checked prior to the hunt.) Since driving is one of the more rugged and vigorous methods of hunting, those who do the "driving" should be in particularly good physical condition.

The hunters line up. They will spread to about 150-feet apart before they enter the heavily wooded drive area.

In organizing the drive it is best to appoint one man as group leader. He should be a veteran hunter, one who knows the area, has good common sense and the capacity to plan well. In case of a dispute or disagreement, or faced with a new situation, he should be depended upon to present sound, sensible and fair decisions. He should know his men well so that he can utilize their capabilities. Some hunters may only want to "post;" others may like to drive and have the physical constitution to bear the strain of it. Ordinarily, if there are more drives than one per day, the "drivers" and "posters" will alternate their roles. In an eleven hour period—daybreak to dusk—as many as four to eight drives may be carried out, depending on the terrain, the pace of the "drivers," the success of the drive and how far the various drive areas are from each other. Usually they are quite close, so the latter is no problem. However, part of the group may have to be driven to their new area to set up a new drive-line and/or be assigned new posts.

The group leader, in a spirit of cooperation with the other hunters, organizes all the drives. He must explain clearly and carefully all the details. The specific "posting" and starting assignments and the drive-line must be discussed. Using a regional map or a sketch of the area, the group leader shows each individual his zone of action. Still more ideal would be a visit to the area with a "dry run" if possible. All individuals should be aware of the starting assignments and the positions of all the other members.

The group members are divided as we have seen into two companies—the "drivers" and the "posters." The leader of the whole group will usually act as the captain of the "drivers" and one of the "posters" is appointed captain of the latter group. The two captains can maintain liaison throughout the hunt by using walkie-talkies. As you can see in the schematic, the "drivers" are from 150 to 200 feet apart and the distance of the drive is approximately one mile. The danger line is an imaginary line—the three-quarter point. Once the "drivers" have left Area A they no longer shoot in the direction of the "posters." Stating this in another way, once the "drivers" are in Area B, they shoot only in the direction of Area A. Drives are safe but they also require a lot of common sense. As we have already stated, a deer stands only

A "poster" on the alert—a deer may appear at any moment.

A deer is easily camouflaged—be alert!

Speed is essential. Don't hesitate.

He's down! Let your companions know you got him.

thirty six inches high. The standing hunter will automatically be shooting in a downward position with the rifle angled safely toward the ground.

D-Day now arrives. All have assumed their positions. By prearranged signal, such as a shot at a specified time or by walkie-talkie, the hunt is started from the drive-line. Aroused or spooked deer do not follow any prescribed course. They may run straight ahead for a short distance and stop, or they may gradually circle back to the area from which they started. Or they may run straight ahead for a long distance. "Posters" must remain standing and on the alert, for a deer can run the mile distance in less than two minutes. The "drivers" advance steadily in a zig-zag ïashion, yelling and shouting and trying by their noise to arouse the deer from their beds. At this time, the more noise the better. As the "drivers" walk through the woods, they kick at every large bush and at the bases of the larger trees. Deer sleep in "bedded down" areas and hide in bushes, under trees or alongside rocks. At times, a deer will play "possum" and lie still until you are right upon him or touch him. Once he is on the move, however, he can leap a roadway or jump over a car in one bound. So be on guard every second. It is not unusual to shoot a deer as close as ten foot ahead, while on a drive.

The drive continues onward. Drivers #1 and #4 besides driving effect a type of flanking movement which helps to keep the deer in the drive area. If a "driver" shoots a deer, he approaches it with caution and makes certain that it is dead. He stays with his deer and notifies the others of his success. Incidentally, "drivers" will generally kill just as many deers as the "posters"

The "drivers" continue to move forward and across the danger line. But now they shoot *only* at deer who have passed them and are moving toward the direction of the original drive line. The "posters" may fire in the direction of the drive-line only until the "drivers" have reached the danger line, about three quarters of the total distance to be covered. This information is obtained by direct sighting, or by use of walkie-talkie between "drivers" and "posters." Any deer that go out of Area B and past the "posters" now become safe and suitable targets for the "posters." Deer that head back toward Area A past the "drivers" become safe and suitable targets for the "drivers." A situation could arise, particularly near the end of the drive, when a deer could be midway between the "drivers" and the "posters" and is sighted by both. *Neither* shoots until the deer makes its move—either past the "drivers" or past the "posters." Then and only then is the *safe* shot taken. When the distance between the "drivers" and the "posters" is less than one quarter of a mile, neither "posters" nor "drivers" fire in the direction of one another. This is the danger zone.

Those who are posted *never* leave their assigned positions until the drive is finished. Their safety is assured if they *stand fast*. If, during the course of the hunt, they shoot a deer and it is downed, they should wait until the drive is completed before the deer is approached. If the deer is hit and runs away the "drivers" may see it again. If it is not downed by the "drivers" its course may be followed *after* the drive is finished.

In summary, four elements tend to make the drive a safe procedure. They are:

1. The maintenance of good communications both laterally, as well as between "drivers" and "posters" so the positions of all involved are always known.

2. The constant and unchanging position of the "posters" from the beginning to the end of the drive.

3. Deer are of such a size that a shot by a hunter in an upright position is made at a downward angle.

4. Once the "drivers" reach the danger zone they no longer shoot toward the "posters." The only deer that the "drivers" may now shoot are deer that have passed them and are going back toward Area A. Therefore, they will now be shooting toward the area they have just covered.

One other safety factor is that the more dense the woods the more protection from stray or ricocheting shots is given by the trees themselves.

We expect the hunt to be successful. Now the ones who made their kill are helped with the field dressing and transportation problem. Time becomes an important factor—particularly for those who did not get their deer. So, as soon as possible, start the next drive for which you have already planned. Start each drive with a fresh and optimistic spirit. Remember that darkness descends rapidly, and the hunters should be on the roads or in the cars by that time. The time consumed in changing from one area to a new one and in transporting the deer has to be considered in order to avoid moving about the woods at night.

12. FURTHER FACTS ON HUNTING

THE WHITE-TAILED DEER

The white-tailed deer is hunted in New York State by 575,000 registered deer hunters with about 95,000 deer killed in 1969. This means that 480,000 did not get a deer or that only one out of six hunters was successful. The estimated deer population in New York State is approximately 370,000 to 380,000. As you can see, the deer are there but you have to work to get them. The more you learn about the sport, the better your chances of success. The statistics above can be changed by more knowledge and training.

The life expectancy of a male deer in New York State is one to two years of age. Yet, it is not unusual to see, at the checking station, deer seven, eight or nine years of age. It may be helpful, on your next visit to your checking stations, to practise determining the deer's age. Help will often be given cheerfully by those in charge.

The term "aging" the deer is used loosely and means to determine the age of the deer. The type of and degree of teeth maturity give the chief clues to the deer's age. The first molar appears at six months of age. The presence of deciduous (baby) teeth and degree of replacement by permanent ones will shed light on whether the deer is two years old or under, for at two years the third molar appears. By three years of age, all the teeth are mature. By the age of ten, the teeth may be worn down to the gum line.

Determining the age is not so important at this time. But it is a necessity when cooking time comes, as the venison is handled differently depending on the age of the deer.

In some states only bucks—male deer, with antlers three inches long or longer—may be shot. The size of the rack gives no indication of the age of the deer, since antlers are shed in December of every year. The size only gives evidence of good or bad nutrition in the previous year. If the nutrition was good—for example, apples and corn—the antlers will be large and many pointed. A twelve point buck could be a spike buck in the following year, if it is forced to move to a poor browsing area or if the deer are so plentiful that browsing is generally poor.

Occasionally these dropped antlers may be found in the woods. The average deer in New York weighs between eighty to one hundred and thirty pounds, but the one hundred thirty pounders are few and far between. The biggest deer that I, personally, weighed was two hundred and two pounds (after field dressing),

Joe Sr. shows Joe Jr. the difference in antlers.

and it came from Canada. So, if you do shoot a deer, don't be disappointed if it is small. Remember, there are hundreds of thousands of hunters who didn't get any at all.

Deer tend to be curious even when they are being chased. Many times if you yell at them, they will be startled, stop, and become a good target. Naturally, a standing deer makes a better target than a moving one. Bucks generally travel by themselves. Does and fawns usually travel together. Incidentally, many experts tend to believe that a deer's sense of smell is acute. However, my own experience would not tend to bear this out. I have seen deer approach a hunter who was smoking a cheap cigar. I have seen deer approach hunters both downwind and upwind. Buck lures have never proven their effectiveness to me, and buck whistles fall into the same category. In talking to thousands of hunters annually, this seems to be the consensus of opinion. Rather than using lures and whistles, it is much more important to know the pattern of deer behavior.

The various types of deer in different sections of the country should be studied carefully. The behavior pattern would include such items as where the deer hide when under pursuit and pressure and where they go in heavy snow or rain. Other factors such as browsing habits and where they tend to lie and bed down have to be considered. Let us now discuss these points in regard to the white-tailed deer.

Weather conditions are one of the most important factors to be considered when planning a hunting trip.

HUNTING IN THE RAIN

Deer are no different from human beings. What is the first thing you do when it starts to rain? You head for shelter—so do they. Hunting in the rain is one of the best times to hunt, as your search can be shortened with a little common sense. Some veteran hunters believe that deer head for the hills during a storm, but I tend to disagree. I believe that, when the first shot is fired on the opening day of the deer hunting season, deer head for safety the same place they go for shelter when it's raining, snowing or sleeting—"the pines." These are dense patches of evergreen trees which, although they can grow to great height, often have branches which grow close to the ground providing many good hiding places for deer. These piney patches may be small, sometimes only ten feet square, or they may extend for a couple of miles. Hunting "the pines" can be very rugged as the branches sometimes seem to grow together because of the thickness of growth. Occasionally, a hunter will have to crawl on hands and knees to "spook" the deer. It is usually dry in "the pines" so the deer will bed down there day and night. In various hunting trips, when we have killed the deer in "the pines," their skins were completely dry despite a heavy, prolonged rainfall. Some deer will stay in these areas all day, as long as they're not disturbed. At night they come out to hunt for food. I have seen a deer hiding underneath a pine tree that had a spread of only four feet, while many hunters failed to sight it and passed right by. It was only when one of the hunters accidentally tripped on a branch that the deer, to everyone's amazement, leaped out.

Deer will also hide in the swamp areas because there are isolated dry sections where pine trees grow. They may also be found hiding in laurels and under wild rhododendron plants. Many hunters do not go into the heavily wooded areas, preferring to follow the easiest routes. This approach, however, produces very few deer. Hunting "the pines" can be easy if you and your party are on a drive through the trees.

The pines can be "driven" with only one other hunting partner, too. An old trick I use when hunting with a small group is to bring along a small portable radio. While my buddy covers the outside of "the pines" in an open area, I walk and sometimes crawl through the other side with the volume of the radio turned up high. Deer will jump from their beds and run when awakened by loud noises. When a deer is on the move, everyone in the woods has a chance to shoot him. When he crosses an open field, which occasionally happens, you can well believe he was chased from "the pines."

I know hunters who haven't shot a deer in fifteen years. After talking to them, I learned that they stand in fields all day, hide in apple orchards, sit in back of some farm house or wait in corn fields. During the day, while the deer season is on, the deer will not come out in the open. If night hunting were legal, *which it is not,* you would find thousands of deer in these areas at night. But at daybreak they are gone.

Rising at 5:00 A.M. to go hunting in the cold rain is considered foolish by many. But I have never heard a hunter who has waited all year for that one big weekend say, "Let's wait until next year." The majority of hunters stay in motels or camps and sleep or play cards during a rain storm. But the avid hunter dons his rain gear, oils his gun, takes a sandwich and some hot coffee and heads for "the pines" as this is where the action is and this is what he's waited for.

HUNTING IN THE SNOW

Hunting in freshly fallen snow is probably one of the most exciting ways to hunt. It is very easy to spot your deer as he is big and brown and stands out. The hunters in their brightly colored garb stand out as well. Deer can be tracked in the snow because their paths are easy to follow. And, if your shot has only wounded your deer and he runs off, you can easily follow his blood trail.

In the event your shot was fatal, and you have to drag your deer back to camp, you will be delighted to find that he will slide across the snow covered ground easily. Snow shoes have proven to be a great help in a heavy snowfall. So, no matter what the weather conditions, deer will be found in "the pines," laurels or rhododendrons. These will always be good areas to hunt, for the deer "live" there.

AFTER THE SNOWFALL

When fresh snow lies over all the ground, the deer stands out in sharp contrast. However, as the snow begins to melt, new problems arise. Small patches of snow can look like the tail of the deer, patches of brown earth can simulate the deer in a reclining position and the bare branches of a tree or bush can seem like antlers. Imagination must be kept under control for it is easy to see a deer where none exists. Tracks are much harder to follow where there are patches of snow alternating with large areas of bare ground.

45

The sloppy type of underfooting which develops with the melting snow also creates new difficulties. It is harder to keep up the pace of trying to follow the deer. A slip or fall may cause injury or, if your gun is 'at the ready,' may cause your gun to fire. So in this situation, be extremely careful. In stalking deer or in maintaining a sitting or "posting" position, the ground underfoot will be much less likely to sound any warning. This is probably the only advantage of hunting after the snow.

FROZEN CONDITIONS

Many times, while hunting for the white-tailed deer, you will encounter freezing weather and frozen ground. Keeping yourself warm is difficult enough, but the problem of walking over partly frozen ground that with every step makes a loud crunching noise that can be heard for hundreds of yards makes stalking almost impossible. Also, in cold weather, deer tend to be more active and you are more apt to see them on the move. With the temperature dropped to zero, stalking, standing or just sitting for any length of time usually gets to be too uncomfortable to tolerate easily. The hunter and the deer must move just to keep warm. Special hand warmers, battery-heated socks, insulated boots, extra clothing, heater-type cushions, etc., may be used if indicated. Close communication between all members of a hunting party is important at all times, but particularly during bitter cold weather. If you intend to leave the hunting area, be sure your decision is known to others in your group, lest time be wasted looking for a "lost" hunter.

WARM WEATHER

Occasionally during the deer season the temperature will rise to fifty or sixty degrees. The deer definitely tend to move about less and you may have to force them from their beds. They may also be found browsing and moving about slowly in the woods. Warm weather will naturally require less clothing, so suitable measures should be taken. However, you must remember that, if you down your deer while the temperature is above forty-five degrees, your deer must be handled quickly and properly or the venison will become spoiled.

46

TIME OF DAY

Many people have asked me, "What is the best time to hunt?" Generally, it is believed that daybreak and just before dusk are two of the best times. I tend to agree with this but, in actuality, any time is a good time for the smart hunter. If the deer are out there and you have the right crew and the energy and the enthusiasm, you can "push" the deer into the open. With vigor and interest, you can control the circumstances. If you are more passive in nature, then circumstances will control you. While talking to thousands of hunters in the past ten years, I have found that most of their deer were shot between 10 a.m. and 4:00 p.m. Without a doubt, luck does play a role, but planned, intelligent activity plays even a greater role.

Included in this section will be a brief discussion of deer paths, deer trails, deer crossings, deer tracks and droppings.

A deer path is a route frequently followed by one or two deer. The area will be bare and beaten down with definite tracks in evidence.

A deer crossing is an area where trails or paths cross each other. A smart hunter is well aware that these paths, etc., are made during the summer months. They are a good sign in the late summer and early fall that this area is where the deer are to be found in the coming deer season. But with the first shot, the whole pattern of activity and the use of these trails can change suddenly.

The deer now avoids the routes that he had previously walked freely. Rarely will he walk along his old trail. The hunter who waits for him there may have a long wait indeed. I have talked to hunters who have waited by deer trails, or in stands along deer paths —with no success. Some have been "hunting" for eight to ten years and still have not seen their first deer.

While information about paths and trails is helpful, it must be remembered that they were made months before the season opened. Deer droppings can, however, provide more recent clues as to the number of deer in the area as well as to their very presence. It is important to learn to distinguish between old and fresh droppings. The former are firm and dull, while the latter are soft, shiny and, if very recent, may even be "smoking." This would mean the deer is only minutes away.

Examination of tracks and following same is not too helpful for the average hunter except in newly fallen snow. Even though these signs are helpful, too much time is usually wasted trying to evaluate the tracks and droppings. It is perhaps of greater value to try and figure out where the deer may be headed or where he might be seeking cover than to slowly follow his trail. Remember, the droppings may be "fresh" but the deer may be three miles away.

FINAL OBSERVATIONS

Deer hunters should be alert every moment they are in the woods. Any movement whatsoever should arouse great interest. A pheasant or partridge flying up in front of you may mean that no hunter is ahead of you and that you are walking into "fresh" territory. It may mean that deer are on the run in front of you. What you might first think is a squirrel at fifty yards or a rabbit running through the woods may on a careful second look turn out to be a deer. A deer can crawl between logs and all you may see is part of his tail and back. He might appear like a rabbit or a fox. At two or three hundred yards, a deer can even look like a dog.

The white-tailed deer runs with his head and tail held high. The tail is often called the "flag." When the deer is wounded however, the tail drops (the flag is down). This is one of the first signs he is in trouble.

As far as the success of the hunt, a lot may depend on the number of hunters involved. Generally, the more hunters that are trudging through the woods and the more thorough they are in "spooking" the deer, the better the hunting will be for all concerned. More deer on the move means more opportunity to get a shot at them. A deer ranging over a wide area may be seen by twenty five or thirty or even more hunters.

Some hunters still tend to believe that deer can perceive color and interpret the significance of a blaze-orange or bright red jacket as a threat to them. I strongly challenge this belief. I have had a few deer come up and almost "kiss" me, even though I was dressed in regular bright hunting apparel. The color did not deter them in the slightest from approaching me. However, the slightest move on my part seemed to startle them and off they would

48

bound. It is more logical that the perception of movement is one of the first things that will make a deer run for safety.

I personally do not think the deer's sense of smell is very acute. After all, I have had them come within touching distance. If their sense of smell were such a protective device, why would they continue to roam the hunted area? The ability to use natural cover to its best advantage and its speed are the deer's best defensive weapons. Unfortunately, their curiosity and their failure to appreciate fully the dangerous position in which they find themselves often lead to their downfall. With their speed and sense of awareness of man's presence, they should be, theoretically, much more difficult to down. For one standing at "post," it is important not to move at all once a deer has been detected. It may approach even closer, allowing for a more favorable shot.

Associated with the privilege of hunting there are many rules and regulations to guarantee that these privileges are not abused. The various states and conservation departments set up guidelines that must be followed for the good of all concerned. The rules are strict and the penalties are often severe. It is absolutely imperative that all of these regulations be fully known by the hunter and followed by him.

In both a sense of fairness and in a spirit of cooperation, those rules forbidding transportation of a loaded rifle or shot-gun in a car, hunting at night, or shooting from a car should be obeyed. The individual laws should be reviewed. In most states it is necessary to tag your deer at the earliest opportunity after you have downed your deer. The tag should be firmly attached, so that when you are dragging your deer the tag does not come loose. Heavy fines or loss of your deer would result if you lose the tag. More severe penalties such as a $1,000 fine, loss of your rifle and even the automobile may follow more serious infractions. All aspects of the hunt should be thoroughly understood, such as party permits, "doe days," and the proper transportation of the deer. In this regard, a part of the deer has to be exposed during the drive home. Once again review your local hunting laws. Laws are made to be followed—not to be broken.

While we are discussing laws, we might call to mind the fact that there is a certain tendency in our land to create more rigid

49

anti-gun laws. By keeping in touch with your local hunting club, you will be informed of new legislation. As you read your daily paper, you will notice the pressures being put on our lawmakers in regard to gun control. It is important for us as citizens and as hunters to stand up for our rights and to try and maintain the privileges of hunting. (The National Rifle Association has been an outstanding defense force in this fight and it should be congratulated. It has made a tremendous and continuing effort to create interest in the rifle and similar guns, while being in the forefront in its drive for safety and the proper handling of the rifle. I personally urge and enthusiastically recommend that every hunter join the N.R.A. By being a member, you can be kept informed on many aspects of hunting, shooting, ammunition, safety techniques as well as new gun legislation.)

Most deer are killed within two miles of the road. Before the season, hundreds may be seen along the roads in the orchards and backyards or in the fields lying in the sun. With the first shot of the season, they mysteriously disappear. From then on, to get one, you have to earn it.

13. DOWNING THE DEER

Seven thirty Monday morning—D-Day. The sun is just starting its climb. You are standing alertly at your post. A shot rings out and the sound reverberates over the hills. The drive is on. You hear the voice of the lead-driver over your walkie-talkie, shouting, "Here we come." You tense up. Your pulse begins to race. The moment you had planned for and looked forward to with such great anticipation is now at hand. In a minute or two a deer could be running toward you. Anxiety mounts. You brace yourself against a tree. Your breath comes more quickly and you can feel a slight tremor of your arms. Your eyes search the field ahead, watching for the slightest movement. "What was that?" Your eyes strain and all your muscles grow taut. "Was that a rabbit? No, A deer? A deer! Off with the safety. Where did the deer go? There it is. It's coming closer—closer. About one hundred yards now. Wait—wait! It's turning. Seventy five yards. Perfect! Steady now. Aim—careful. Shoot."

"I got it—I got it. It's down. It's not moving. Wait. Watch it. If I were a "driver" I would be out there now. Patience. The driv-

ers will come. The deer isn't moving." At last the drivers are
sighted. You yell to them "I got one over here." Approach it with
caution with the gun 'at the ready.'

There is no movement. You are ready for a shot to the back of
the neck but it is not necessary. No unnecessary shots to ruin the
meat. You see that your shot, since it hit in the heart section, was
effective at once.

The deer is down. Congratulations pour out from your buddies. You smile and laugh and begin to tell the story for the first
of thousands of times. This is hunting. This is living.

Approach with caution.

14. FIELD-DRESSING THE DEER

A few seasons ago I heard a shot on a ridge and walked up to find
a hunter standing over a fine, fat, young buck. We stood there
admiring the animal as the hunter told with dramatic detail, how
he had downed this, his first deer. Then he stopped short, looked
at me and said, "What the devil do I do with it, now that I've got
it?" That question comes to many hunters each year after they
have fired the fatal shot.

Field-dressing is the most important and delicate part of your
trip. Many hunters have done it but very few of them know all the
aspects of it. The flavor of the meat in most cases depends upon
the manner in which your deer is field-dressed. Now that you are
standing beside your deer, if you do not have a blaze-orange
cloth, take off your blaze-orange jacket and drape it over the
rack, the side of the deer or over overhanging brush. And now—
to field-dressing.

A deer should be "dressed out" in the exact spot in which he
was downed. Do not drag him as this causes hem-
orrhaging. Run your fingers down the breast bone of the deer until you reach the first part of the soft upper belly. At this point just
below the breast bone insert the point of your knife. Pene-

trate the skin completely, about 1/4 inch or so, but not so deeply as to cut the intestines. Make a small cut approximately 1/2 inch extension and step back. Most of the time gas will escape from the deer with a hissing sound. This gas sometimes has a foul odor. While the gas escapes, roll up your sleeves and put on your disposable gloves. This will protect you from ticks and infection and make the process much more sanitary. The plastic bag which held the throw-away gloves can now be used to hold the heart, liver and kidneys of your deer. Wait another minute to be sure that most of the gas has escaped, then re-insert your knife and extend the incision the whole length of the belly wall down to the pelvis. If the belly wall is pulled toward you and the sharp edge of the knife is faced away from the intestines, there will be little chance of cutting these intestines, but be careful of your own fingers! The intestines will then be exposed and will fall out of the belly. Put your hand into the cavity and over the liver. Pull down on the liver which lies mostly on the right side of the deer. This will expose the diaphragm, a smooth muscle that separates the chest cavity from the abdominal cavity. Cut the diaphragm, where it is attached to the lower ribs, in a circular manner. Now you place your hand into the chest cavity and over the heart. Pull down firmly on the heart. Now, with your knife, go as high as possible into the chest cavity up to the neck region. Cut across the windpipe (trachea) and the feeding tube (esophagus) which lies behind the windpipe. Gradually cut all the attachments of the heart and pull out the chest contents. Detach the heart and liver and put them in the polyethylene bag. The attachments of the intestines to the back wall of the deer are either pulled loose or cut. The kidneys (bean shaped) will be easily seen and removed. They too are now put in the plastic bag. Do not cut the neck to bleed the deer, as all the blood will later be drained out when the deer is hung. The intestines are now only attached to the body by the rectal tube. It is very important that this tube be completely and cleanly removed. Below the base of the tail, the opening (vent) of the rectal tube will be seen. This should be widely encircled (3 inch diameter) with the knife deeply inserted to a depth of at least 5 inches. Encircle at least two or three times. At this point, insert your hand inside the deer and pull firmly on the rectal tube. It may be loose, but if it remains attached, cut around the tube from the inside to release it completely. As you can see, the new opening that has been made is at least three inches in diameter and will serve as a "drain" for the blood when the deer is hung head high.

At this point, step behind the deer and tilt it away from you in order to drain out of the cavity as much blood as possible. This should be done quickly because blood congeals rapidly. Your deer is now properly field-dressed. Now take off and discard your disposable gloves; place the bag (with liver, kidneys and heart) into the pocket of your jacket and you are ready to return to camp.

Under Joe DeFalco's watchful eye, a successful hunter begins the field-dressing procedure.

SCENT OR MUSK GLANDS

Some hunters and experts believe that the scent or musk glands located in the hind legs of deer must be removed. It is so stated in many books, and thousands of hunters have asked me about them and how to remove them.

I firmly believe that the "experts" tend to be wrong in this matter. I was considered a food expert in the Army and, during many months spent in the slaughter houses of Chicago, I observed the processing of thousands of animals. If it were necessary to remove these glands from deer, they would also have to be removed from pigs, lambs, calves and steer. And this is not done. On many occasions, I have personally removed these glands, but found no difference in the taste of the meat. The United States Government spends millions of dollars on research in order to ensure that the food on your table is of the highest quality. At no time has there been any specific advice given that these glands be removed. Until the United States Government or some scientist presents specific evidence to the contrary, I will continue to leave the scent glands in the legs.

The illustrations on the following pages are in sequence throughout the entire field-dressing procedure. You will find it quite simple if you follow these instructions.

Just below the breast bone.

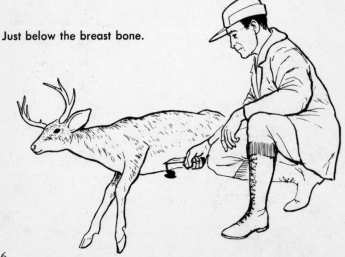

Put on your disposable gloves while the gas escapes.

Continue down to pelvic bone.

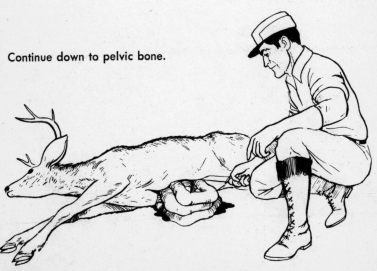

57

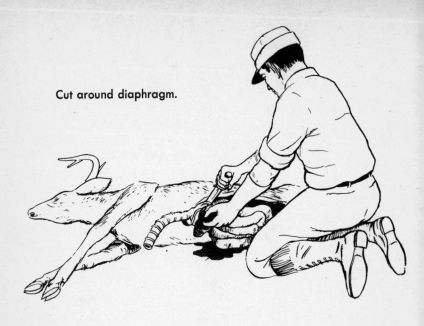

Cut around diaphragm.

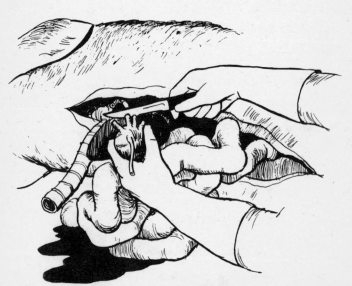

Separate heart, liver and kidneys.

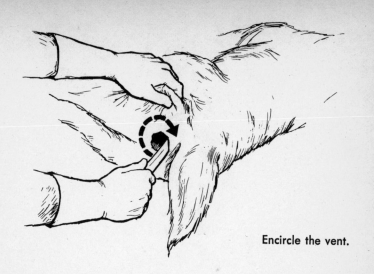

Encircle the vent.

Encircle the vent from inside, remove the tube.

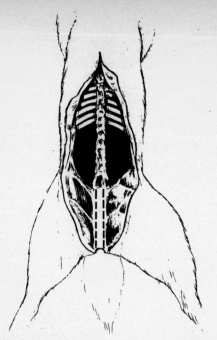

Vent tube is removed from this area.

Drain out all blood.

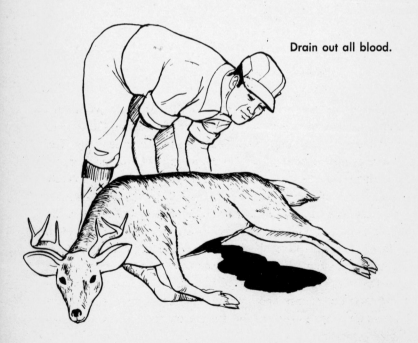

15. THE RETURN TO CAMP

The deer has been field-dressed, your hunting companions have been summoned and now the problem of dragging the deer to camp arises. The shortest way may not be the easiest way. The blaze-orange or bright red cover cloth is placed over the deer and is fastened to hoofs and antlers. Decked out like this, it is unlikely that your deer may be mistaken for a live target by other hunters. A dead buck should be dragged by the antlers and a doe by the rear legs. A large deer will almost always take at least two men to drag it, without too much strain on either. Drag your deer about fifty feet at a time. If it is a trophy buck, try not to abuse the head and neck as they are required in mounting. Avoid rocks, projecting roots and stumps and avoid areas where there may be abrupt step-like drops in the terrain. Do not try to be heroic, learn to pace yourself.

If the country is particularly mountainous, the ground rough and rocky, or if it is important that no damage occur to the deer-skin, then the pole-carry is used. Find a sturdy branch six to eight feet long. Tie the front legs together and tie the rear legs together. Run the pole between the legs and tie the legs and the head to the pole. This latter step prevents the head from swaying from side to side. The pole is placed on the shoulders for carrying and the trip to camp begins. Go slowly, for it is quite a strenuous task. In some areas, you can get a jeep, a tractor or even a horse to help with the task.

On returning to camp, hang your deer in the shade with its head end high and the rear legs at least three to four feet off the ground. Scavengers, dogs and varmits will be less likely to eat the meat from the legs when they are at this height. It is best to hang the deer near your tent or house so it can be kept in view. Deer are occasionally stolen after they have been field-dressed and hung. They make a good prize after most of the work has been done.

After three or four hours of hanging the blood will stop drain-ing. Take your knife and cut away about three inches of the flank on both sides. It is worthless, so you are not losing any meat. The flank begins at the margin of the rib cage and continues down to the pelvis bone. The final opening will be approximately seven to nine inches in width by thirty six inches in length. This opening is essential for air circulation.

Take a handful of salt and throw it into one half pail of water. Use this salt solution to wash out the cavity. Wash out all the old blood so these areas inside the deer are "whistle clean." After this, the cavity is dried with a clean cloth. Within an hour, the ribs inside the "cage" will be shiny.

Never hang your deer in the sun. The coolest place should be used. If the temperature rises over forty five degrees, put the deer in the coldest part of your camp or house (cellar or shed). Warm temperatures can ruin your deer quickly. If the temperature is fifty five or sixty degrees, you are better off breaking camp and going home early. Don't skin the deer at any time unless you plan to cut it up and freeze it at once. The deer is now ready to transport home.

Dragging a deer to camp is a big job—if at all possible use the buddy system.

Hang him head high.

Cut away the flanks.

Wash the cavity out thoroughly.

Dry the cavity.

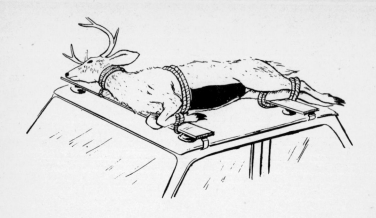

16. TRANSPORTING THE DEER

Prior to the trip, it is a wise investment to buy a sturdy roof rack. The deer should be kept cool at all times, from the moment it is shot until it is prepared for the freezer, and the circulation of air is good on the roof. Only as a second choice should the trunk of the car be used to transport deer. With the aid of two or three of your buddies, the deer is raised to its position on the rack and lashed firmly to it. If the deer is exceptionally large, or if there are two or three deer, it is somewhat safer to run the cord around the roof completely (with the cord actually going inside the car). If there are two or more deer, the antlers of each may be tied together and the deer fastened individually to the rack as well as bound to each other.

On the way home, check the deer every twenty miles to be sure they are not shifting positions. If it is necessary to stop at a diner on the way home, park the car in a cool place and keep the deer in view. At times, deer have been stolen while the successful hunters boasted of their prowess. If necessary, one hunter may have to stand guard over the deer.

If on returning home, the outside temperature is about forty to forty five degrees, hang the deer head high from a branch of a tree. If the temperature is higher than this, a cellar floor that is cold or a cold garage floor may be used. If the temperature rises above fifty degrees, skin the deer and prepare it for the freezer.

17. SKINNING THE DEER

Prior to butchering, and cutting the venison into steaks, chops and roasts, the skin must be removed. The tools necessary for this procedure are a boning knife, a meat saw (or hack saw) and two hooks, placed about two feet apart, for hanging.

The main steps to skinning your deer are illustrated in sequence on the following pages.

Step   1. With the deer on the floor, saw off the hind legs one inch below the kneecap.

Step   2. Saw off the front legs two inches above the knees, through both meat and bone.

Step   3. Using the boning knife, make a hole between the bone and the tendon where it is fixed onto the bone in the back portion of both knees. This is used for hanging the deer.

Step   4. Hang your deer hind leg upward with the hook in the hole in the right leg. This leaves the left leg hanging free.

Step   5. Make a slight cut through the skin of the left hind leg, about six inches below the pelvis. Extend the cut to the bottom of the large tendon called the hock. Do not let your knife cut into the meat. Pull the skin firmly in a downward direction at the same time gradually releasing, with short repeated cuts, the attachments of the skin to the venison.

Step 6. Finish the left leg and continue freeing the skin down to the left shoulder.

Step 7. Now hang the deer by its left leg and repeat the process (steps 5 and 6) removing the skin from the right leg down to the right shoulder.

Step 8. Now that the skin is halfway off, use a second hook and hang right leg as well. Grab skin firmly with both hands and pull down as far as you can, using the point of the knife whenever necessary.

Step 9. The skin is now approximately three quarters of the way off the deer. Step toward the open side of the deer. With your knife, cut into the skin in the upper forward part of the right shoulder down to where the leg has been cut off. Loosen the skin over this leg by pulling on the skin and cutting with the knife (as was done on the hind legs.)

Step 10. Cut the skin from the center of the breast-bone straight down to the level of shoulders (approximately fifteen inches). Never cut below the shoulder level, as this will prevent a perfect mounting of your specimen.

Step 11. Once again using knife and pulling type motion loosen skin that is still fastened to the deer. This would resemble the rolling down of a stocking.

Step 12. Repeat this as far down the neck as possible but do not release the skin close to the head area.

Step 13. Take the knife and make a cut through the meat in the neck approximately one inch from the line where the skin is still attached to the deer. This cut is made as deeply as possible all around the neck.

Step 14. Place the saw blade in this deep incision and saw through the bony areas underneath. This will release the head and neck completely.

The deer is now completely skinned.

If you do not plan to use the head as a trophy, and would like to try my recipe Simmered Deer Tongue, you may now open the head and remove the tongue. If you want both the trophy and the tongue, you might ask the taxidermist to save the tongue for you.

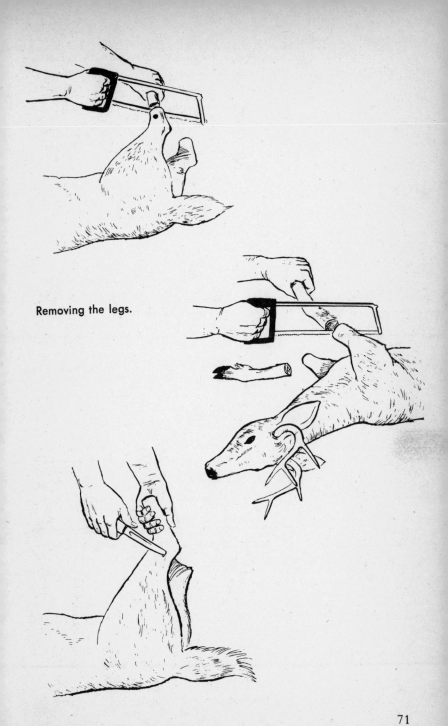

Removing the legs.

Hang it right and make it easy.

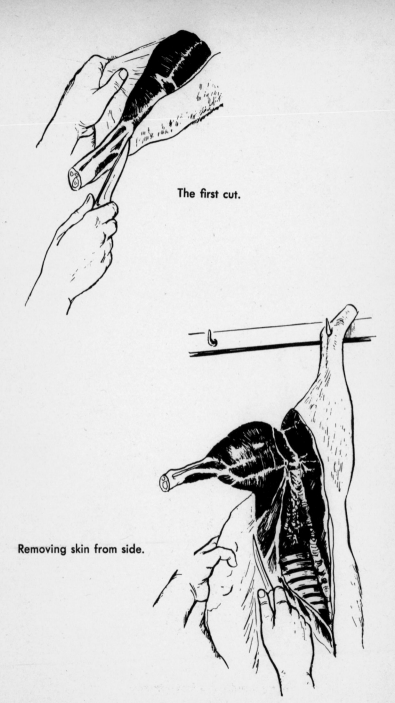

The first cut.

Removing skin from side.

Pulling down the skin.

Removing head and cape.

18.   CARE OF THE TROPHY

IN THE FIELD

From the moment the deer is killed, the head and neck region should receive special care. If a second finishing shot is necessary, it should be placed in the back of the neck. If damage to the head may occur during the return to camp, it is safer to pole-carry the deer, even if it takes two to three hours longer. Temperature changes will affect the head and neck as well as the rest of the deer, so proper attention should be paid to this problem. The sooner the trophy (the head and neck) is in the hands of the taxidermist, the better your chances of getting back a trophy you will be proud to hang prominently on that wall in your den.

As for the other parts of the deer, the hide can be tanned with the hair on to make a rug for the den; or it may be tanned with the hair off to make jackets, gloves and moccasins. From the legs and feet such useful items as lamps, thermometers, gun racks, and foot stools can be made. The body hair is often used for making flies and hair bugs for bass fishing. The tail can be used for streamers or large bucktail jigs for deep sea fishing.

A pocketbook, made from the hide of a deer that you shot, makes a wonderful gift for the wife or girl friend. You may find that when your wife starts talking to her friends about your hunting ability a chain reaction may start. Their husbands may get the message and take up hunting, too!

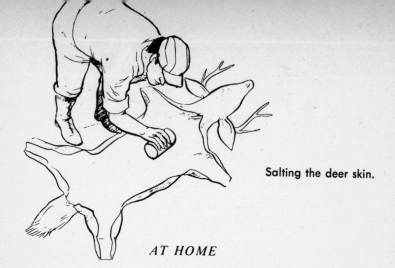

Salting the deer skin.

AT HOME

Now that the skin of the deer and the head are completely released, place on floor as illustrated. Over the inner aspect of skin, distribute uniformly one pound of salt. Use no water. With a circular type of motion use the palm of your hand to work the salt into the skin. Cover all areas including the neck region.

While the skin is still on the floor, fold the legs inward in overlapping fashion (see illustration) and roll up the deerskin. The trophy is now ready for the taxidermist.

Arrangements with the taxidermist should be made as soon as you come home. If, however, you are not able to find a taxidermist to your liking (most are honest and helpful, but there are exceptions) or if the taxidermist you select is too busy at that time to handle your trophy, your deerskin may be kept at home as long as the temperature does not rise above forty five degrees. If the temperature rises, the trophy should be brought to the taxidermist immediately, or *frozen*. Any delay could mean the spoiling or loss of your trophy. The trophy may be kept frozen, i.e. below the freezing point, for a year or two. But once it is thawed and kept for any length of time in warm weather, it is destroyed as a trophy.

Costs for this service vary, so it is better to check with a few taxidermists prior to a final commitment. It generally takes from four to eight months before your trophy is returned, but the trophy is well worth waiting for. It will bring back pleasant memories for years to come.

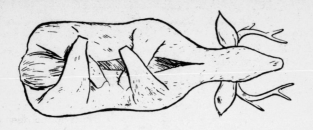

Ready for the taxidermist.

Splitting the deer.

19. BUTCHERING—
CUTS OF MEAT AND LABELING

With the skin completely removed, you can now see where your deer was shot and where the hemorrhage (bleeding) is present in the meat. It is impossible for me to determine how each deer will now be handled since each deer will be a separate problem. The amount of injury and damage and the course of the bullet(s) or arrow(s) will determine the initial steps. Damaged meat, i.e. with old blood on it or with a "sliminess" to the touch, should be thrown away.

In the following steps, we are dealing *theoretically* with a deer that has suffered no damage.

Step 1. With the deer in the hanging position, i.e. just after removal of the skin, cut the deer in half by sawing completely the length of the backbone. The deer is now in two separate sections.

Step 2. Pull the front leg forward and, using a steak knife, remove the shoulder by cutting through the meat on the line where it joins the shoulder base (see complete side chart).

Step 3. Cut the shoulder into three pieces;
    1. Higher shoulder
    2. Lower shoulder
    3. Shank

These pieces should be freezer wrapped and labeled as above for easy reference. Shoulder cuts may be used as chopped meat or for soups, stews and pot roasts.

Step 4. Cut off the hind leg at the loin (see complete side chart).

Step 5. Divide the leg into rump roast, leg steaks or cutlets, shank leg roast and shank (see chart of hind leg). Freezer wrap and label each cut. The roasts may be used as pot roast, roast venison or chopped meat. The shank is used for stew or soup.

Remove shoulder—cut in 3 pieces.

Remove shoulder — cut in 3 pieces.

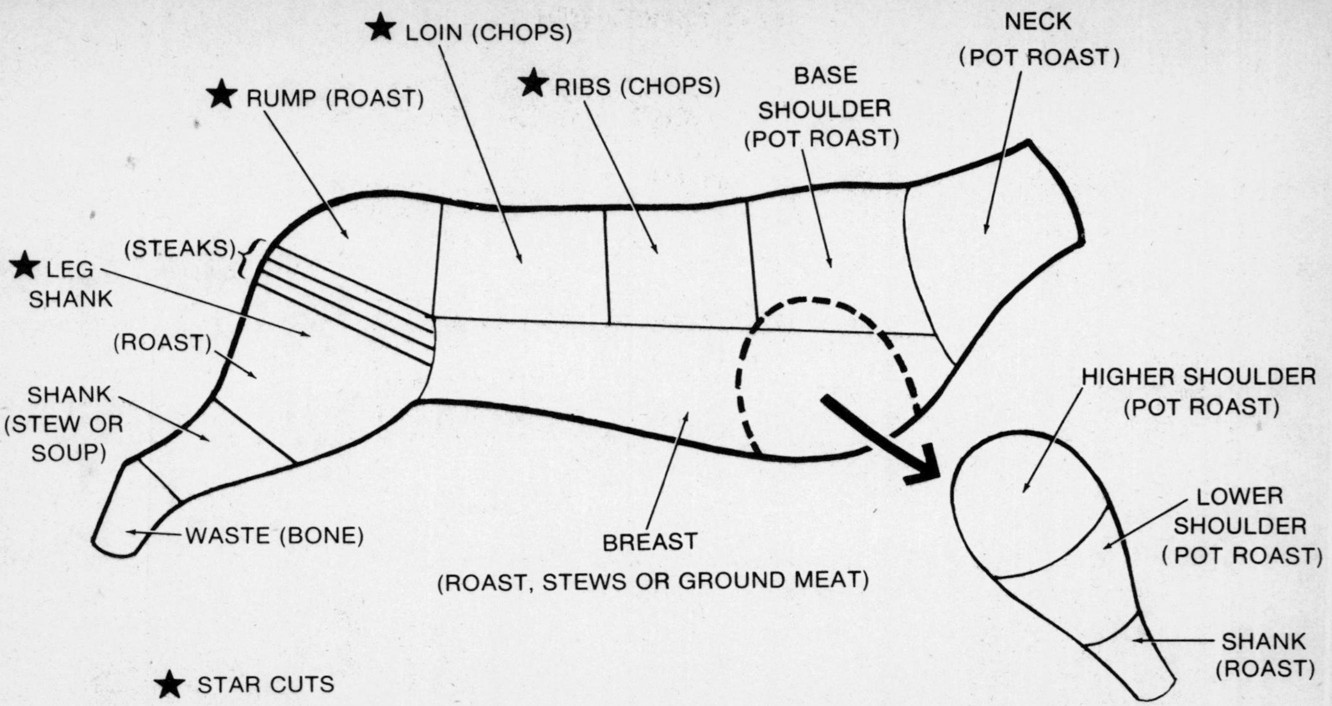

HIGHER SHOULDER (POT ROAST)

LOWER SHOULDER (POT ROAST)

SHANK (ROAST)

NECK (POT ROAST)

BASE SHOULDER (POT ROAST)

★ LOIN (CHOPS)

★ RIBS (CHOPS)

★ RUMP (ROAST)

LEG (STEAKS)

SHANK (ROAST)

SHANK (STEW OR SOUP)

WASTE (BONE)

BREAST (ROAST, STEWS OR GROUND MEAT)

★ STAR CUTS

COMPLETE SIDE CHART

80

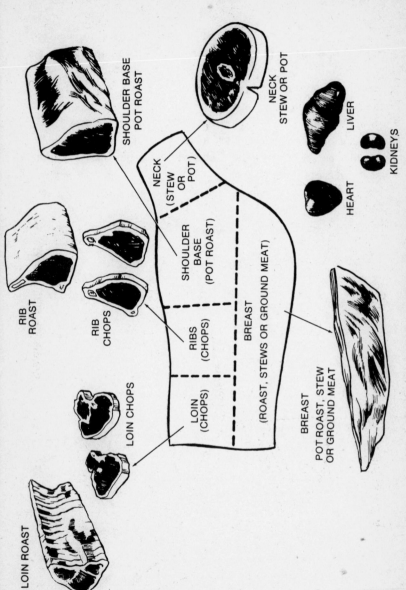

SHOULDER BASE
POT ROAST

NECK
STEW OR POT

LIVER

KIDNEYS

HEART

RIB
ROAST

RIB
CHOPS

NECK
(STEW
OR
POT)

SHOULDER
BASE
(POT ROAST)

RIBS
(CHOPS)

BREAST
(ROAST, STEWS OR GROUND MEAT)

BREAST

POT ROAST, STEW
OR GROUND MEAT

LOIN CHOPS

LOIN
(CHOPS)

LOIN ROAST

FORE QUARTER CHART

81

Step 6. Remove the breast (see forequarter chart). Breast is good for stew, pot roast and ground meat. Freezer wrap and label.

Step 7. Remove the loin and rib sections (see forequarter chart) with knife and cleaver or saw. Separate into loin and ribs. Cracked on the bottom, either loin or ribs may be used as roasts. If desired, chops may be cut from either loin or ribs to be used as chops or steaks (as illustrated).

Step 8. Shoulder base (see forequarter chart) is removed with saw and cleaver. This will leave the neck fully separated. The shoulder base is used for stew, chopped meat, pot roast and soup meat. Freezer wrap and label.

Step 9. The neck can be cut for stew, soups, or boned for chopped meat. Freezer wrap and label.

Step 10. Heart, liver and kidneys must also be freezer wrapped and labeled.

The above steps have been for only one side of the animal. Repeat the steps for the other side. If there is any portion of the deer meat that is too damaged with hemorrhage (bleeding), slimi-

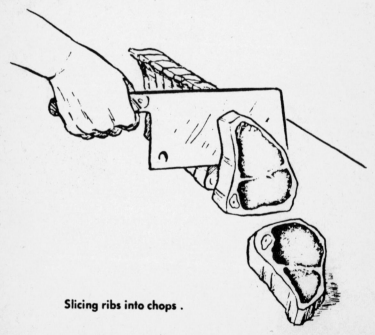

Slicing ribs into chops .

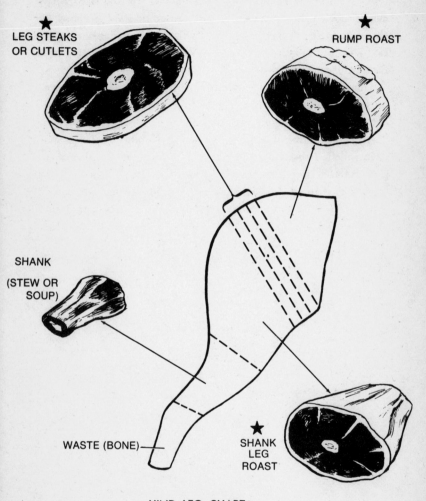

★
**LEG STEAKS
OR CUTLETS**

★
RUMP ROAST

SHANK

**(STEW OR
SOUP)**

WASTE (BONE)

★
**SHANK
LEG
ROAST**

HIND LEG CHART

83

ness or foul odor, throw away at once. If the deer has been field-dressed well and directions followed carefully, there is no reason for any foul odor.

All the above venison should be double wrapped in freezer paper and labeled. Leg steaks, leg roasts, rump roasts, loin chops, rib roasts and cutlets may be marked with a star or special designation as these are the better cuts. Venison can be stored in the freezer for one year.

These steps are fairly easy to follow. However, if you request it, most local butchers are willing to do a more professional job of cutting up and packaging your deer at a reasonable price.

Although quite rare, there is also a possibility that you may have killed a diseased deer. While skinning, if a yellowish or greenish area of pus is noticed or while field-dressing the deer the liver is seen to be spotted, this deer should be checked by food experts or by an experienced butcher/hunter who cuts deer often.

20.   KNOWLEDGE BEFORE COOKING

The white-tailed deer is one of the most hunted animals in the United States. It is also one of the most useful, as every part of the animal can be eaten. Indians lived on venison for many years and, in parts of the country, residents and farmers still live on it. Venison, when handled properly, is delicious. It is also a very expensive item. In the Wild Game Market in New York, some cuts of venison sell for as high as five dollars per pound. In some cases, if a hunter stopped to consider how much his last trip had cost him to get his deer, including the expense of his gun and other equipment, he might find that it cost him *over* five dollars a pound. So, considering the price of food today and the expense your trip has cost you, your family should really give venison a fair try.

Venison is not naturally gamey. However, the inexperienced hunter can make it so. The field-dressing of your deer, as I have said before, is the important thing. If the hunter fails to remove all the intestines or doesn't open up the vent properly, thus leaving blood to remain in the deer, he makes the animal smell gamey. If the temperature should rise to over fifty degrees, the foul odor (which some people mistake for gaminess) will worsen. By the time, the hunter gets home and has the deer cut up into steaks and chops, this smell has already embedded itself into the meat. In my experience, ninety-five per cent of the deer killed by hunters are handled improperly somewhere along the line. That is one reason why I felt the need to write this book.

85

Helped by his son Al, Joe DeFalco determines the deer's age for cooking purposes.

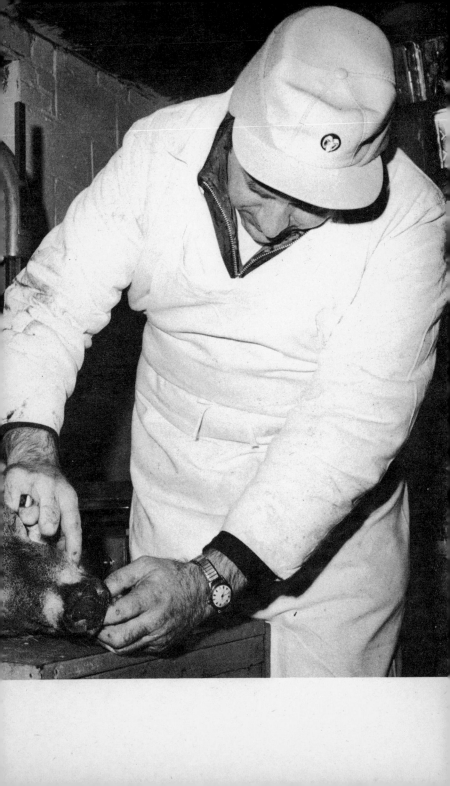

In my career as a hunter and meat expert (I have cut up over fifty-five hundred deer for successful hunters, including fifty of my own), I have heard thousands of stories on how to prepare venison. I have interviewed famous cooks, talked to experienced guides and have read many cookbooks pertaining to venison. Nowhere have I found recipes that specify the age of the deer to be used in the recipes. How can you confidently follow a recipe, when in most cases you are going to be misled? As a butcher, I can assure you that a young doe (female deer) will not eat like a twelve-year-old buck (male deer) that has been roaming the hills. Venison *must* be divided into categories.

The majority of the deer killed are under three years of age. The average deer killed dresses out at less than one hundred pounds of eatable meat. My recipes, which are original and have never been printed before, use every eatable part of the animal. To my knowledge, this has never been done before. The recipes have also been written for both bucks and does under three years of age. As previously stated, the age of your deer can be deter-minded by its teeth. If your deer is older, more cooking time should be allowed. If your deer is a fawn (baby deer of either sex) under six months old, you can follow any preparation for baby lamb. My recipes have been tried by experienced cooks and avid-ly sampled by hundreds of fellow hunters whom I have had the pleasure of hunting with each year. They are different, tasty and delicious. A scale of weights and measures, allowing for your al-teration of the recipes to suit your needs (most of the recipes serve six to eight people), appears on page 115. Remember, all venison should be soaked or washed in salt water prior to cooking in or-der to remove any blood, hair or dirt that may have been left on the meat during packaging.

21. RECIPES

1. Breaded Venison Steaks, Chops or Cutlets
2. Broiled or Griddle Venison Steaks or Chops
3. Venison Patties Griddle or Broiled
4. Venison Italian Sausage with Pork
5. Braised Venison Liver
6. Spiced Venison Pot Roast
7. Venison Goulash
8. Venison Stew
9. Spiced Boneless Stew
10. Venison Ragout
11. Venison Loaf
12. Kidney and Venison Pie
13. Venison Leg Roast
14. Barbecued Venison Hamburgers
15. Venison Meatballs with Pork
16. Venison Curry
17. Diced Venison in Gravy
18. Venison Chops Casserole
19. Venison Sauerbraten
20. Stuffed and Braised Venison Heart
21. Simmered Deer Tongue
22. Venison Cutlets, Italian Style
23. Venison Soup with Vegetables
24. Venison Barbecued on Charcoal
25. Barbecue Sauce for Venison

Recipe #1

BREADED VENISON STEAKS, CHOPS, OR CUTLETS
(use steaks, chops or cutlets)

Ingredients   For 6-8 Servings

Venison with bone .... 5 lbs.
   or
Boneless venison .... 3 1/2 lbs.
Flour, sifted .... 1/2 lb.
Salt .... to taste
Pepper .... to taste
Milk, evaporated .... 4 oz.
Water .... 3 oz.
Eggs, beaten 2
Bread or cracker crumbs .... 4 oz.
Fat .... 4 oz.

Step 1. Cut your venison steaks, chops or cutlets 1/2 inch thick, weighing 3 to 4 ounces each.
2. Mix flour, salt and pepper. Roll venison in flour mixture.
3. Mix milk and water, add beaten eggs. Mix well.
4. Dip floured meat into milk and egg mixture. Dip into crumbs.
5. Brown in a small amount of fat. Stack in baking pans. Cover tightly. Bake in slow oven 325 degrees F. for 45 minutes.

Note— Venison above may also be fried.
Fry until tender in shallow fat, turning frequently to insure even cooking. They may also be fried in deep fat 350 degrees F. approximately 7 to 10 minutes or until done.

90

Recipe #2

BROILED OR GRIDDLE VENISON STEAKS OR CHOPS
(use steaks, chops or cutlets)

Ingredients   For 6-8 Servings

Venison with bone .... 5 lb.
     or
Boneless venison .... 3 1/2 lb.
Salt .... as desired
Pepper .... as desired
Fat .... as desired

Step 1. Cut your venison steaks or chops 3/4 inch thick.
    2. Broil steaks or chops or griddle until brown, turning frequently to insure even cooking.
    3. If meat lacks fat, grease griddle slightly.
    4. Cook to desired degree. Do not overcook.
    5. Sprinkle with salt and pepper just before serving.

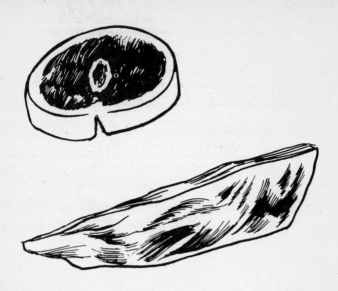

Recipe #3

VENISON PATTIES GRIDDLE OR BROILED
(use neck, shoulders, breast, shanks or legs)

Ingredients   For 6-8 Servings

Boneless venison, ground .... 3 1/2 lb.
Bread crumbs, soft .... 1/4 lb.
Salt .... as desired
Pepper .... as desired
Water .... 5 oz.
Milk .... 3 oz.
Onions, chopped fine .... 1/4 lb.

Step 1. Mix all ingredients together lightly but thoroughly.
   2. Shape into patties 1 in. thick, weighing 3 to 4
oz. each.
   3. Grill or broil about 12 minutes or until cooked
as desired, turning frequently to insure even
cooking.
   4. Serve at once, very hot.

Recipe #4

VENISON ITALIAN SAUSAGE WITH PORK
(use neck, shanks, shoulders or legs)

Ingredients   For 12 Servings

Boneless venison .... 3 lb.
Pork butt .... 3 lb.
Salt .... 2 oz.
Pepper .... as desired
Fennel seeds .... 1 teaspoon
Hog casings .... 4, each approxi-
                                                                 mately 36 in. long
Water or wine sherry .... as directed

Step 1. Grind venison and pork together in home grinder. Use large plate in grinder so it comes out
approximately 1/4 by 1/4. If you don't have a
grinder, this meat can be cut by hand the same
way.

    2. Add salt, pepper and fennel seeds to venison
and pork mixture.

    3. Add wine or water to mixture a little at a time
to moisten. Mix vigorously. When mixture is
moist, stuff into hog casings.

    4. Hog casings should be washed in water inside
and out. The casing can be slipped over a small
home funnel, while you push the ingredients
through. Each sausage link should be about
four inches long, nine links to each casing. Tie
off links and ends with string. (Sausages may be
frozen if desired.)

    5. Fry sausage for about 15 minutes or until done.
Can be used in Italian (spaghetti) sauce as well.

Note— Hog casing can be purchased in any meat
store.

Recipe #5

BRAISED VENISON LIVER

Ingredients   For 6-8 Servings

Deer liver .... from your deer
                                                     average 3 lb.
Flour .... 1/4 lb.
Salt .... as desired
Pepper .... as desired
Fat, bacon .... 1/2 lb.
Water or stock, hot .... as directed

Step 1. Slice liver about 3/8 in. thick. Each piece should
        weigh 4 to 5 oz.
    2. Mix flour, salt and pepper together. Roll liver in
        mixture.
    3. Cook in bacon fat until brown.
    4. Add enough water or stock to cover bottom of
        pan. Cover tightly and cook slowly about 20
        minutes, or until tender, on top of stove.
    5. Chopped onions can be cooked with this if de-
        sired.

Recipe #6

SPICED VENISON POT ROAST
(use shoulders, breast or legs)

Ingredients   For 6-8 Servings

Venison, desired cut	5 lb.
Fat	1 oz.
Salt	as desired
Pepper	as desired
Onions, chopped	1/2 lb.
Vinegar	2 tablespoons
Sour milk or buttermilk	1/2 pint
Water	1/2 pint
Cinnamon	2 sticks

Step 1. Put meat in pan and cook until brown in its own fat or in fat added.

2. Add salt, pepper, onions, vinegar, sour milk, water and cinnamon sticks.

3. Cover tightly and heat to boiling point. Reduce heat and simmer on top of stove or in slow oven 300 degrees F. for 2 hours or until meat is tender, turning meat 2 or 3 times while cooking. Add small amounts of liquid as needed.

4. Remove from pan. Slice in thin slices across grain of meat.

Recipe #7

VENISON GOULASH
(use breast, shoulders, neck, shanks or legs)

Ingredients   For 6-8 Servings

Venison with bone .... 5 lb.
      or
Boneless venison .... 3 1/2 lb.
Onions .... 1/2 lb.
Fat, bacon or beef .... 1/4 lb.
Garlic, ground .... 2 pieces
Marjoram, powdered .... 1/4 teaspoon
Salt .... as desired
Paprika .... 1/4 teaspoon
Flour, sifted .... 1 oz.
Water .... as directed
Tomatoes .... 1 small can

Step 1. Cut meat into 1 in. cubes.
     2. Cook onions in fat until light brown. Add cubed meat and cook until brown. Add boiling water to cover.
     3. Add garlic, marjoram, salt and enough paprika to color red.
     4. Add tomatoes. Cover tightly and heat to boiling point. Reduce heat and simmer about 1 1/2 hours or until meat is tender. Add more liquid if necessary. Drain off surplus liquid.
     5. Mix flour in a small amount of water until smooth. Add this to the liquid. Bring to boiling point and hold for about 2 minutes, stirring constantly.
     6. Combine gravy and meat. Heat to serving temperature and serve.

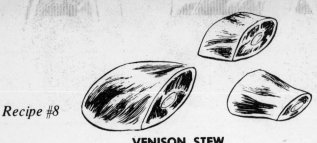

Recipe #8

VENISON STEW
(use neck, shoulders, breast, shanks or legs)

Ingredients	For 6-8 Servings
Boneless venison	3 1/2 lb.
Flour	2 oz.
Salt	as desired
Pepper	as desired
Fat	1/4 lb.
Water	1 pint
Onions, small	1/2 lb.
Carrots, sliced	1/2 lb.
Turnips, sliced	1/2 lb.
Celery, diced	1/2 lb.
Peas, green	1/2 small can
Flour, for gravy	1 tablespoon
Water for gravy	as needed
Tomatoes	small can

Step 1. Cut meat into 1 in. cubes.

2. Mix flour, salt and pepper together. Roll meat in flour and braise in fat until brown.

3. Add water, cover and heat to boiling point. Reduce heat and simmer about 2 hours or until tender. Add vegetables in the following order allowing required time for cooking; onions and carrots 30 minutes; turnips and celery 20 minutes. Drain reserve liquid.

4. Mix flour and water, stirring until smooth. Add to hot meat and vegetables. Heat to boiling point, boil 2 minutes stirring constantly.

5. Pour gravy over meat and vegetables. Reheat and garnish with peas.

6. Add salt and pepper and tomatoes.

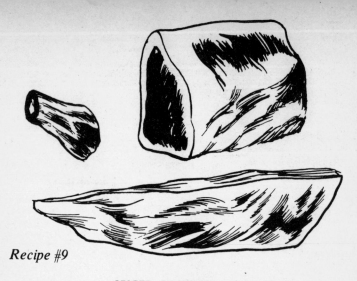

Recipe #9

SPICED BONELESS STEW
(use neck, shoulders, shanks, breast or legs)

Ingredients   For 6-8 Servings

Boneless venison .... 3 1/2 lb.
Flour, sifted .... 2 oz.
Salt .... to taste
Pepper .... to taste
Fat .... 1/4 lb.
Water .... as needed
Vinegar .... 1/4 pint
Brown sugar .... 2 oz.
Cinnamon .... 2 teaspoons
Bay leaves 4
Onions, sliced .... 1/2 lb.

Step 1. Cut meat into 1 1/4 in. cubes.
       2. Mix flour, salt and pepper together. Roll meat in flour and braise in fat until brown.
       3. Add water, cover and heat to boiling point. Reduce heat and simmer 1 1/2 hours until tender.
       4. Mix flour and water, stir until smooth. Add vinegar, brown sugar, cinnamon, bay leaves, onions. Combine all ingredients.
       5. Pour gravy over meat. Add salt and pepper. Reheat and serve.

Recipe #10

VENISON RAGOUT
(use shoulders, neck, shanks, breast or legs)

Ingredients   For 6-8 Servings

Boneless venison .... 3 1/2 lb.
Flour, sifted .... 2 oz.
Salt .... to taste
Pepper .... to taste
Fat .... 1/4 lb.
Water .... as needed
Chopped green peppers .... 1/4 lb.
Worcestershire sauce .... 1/2 teaspoon
Bay leaves 4
Parsley .... sprinkled
Tomatoes .... 1 can # 303
Paprika .... sprinkled
Onions .... ½ lb.

Step 1. Cut meat in 1 in. cubes.
2. Mix flour, salt and pepper together. Roll meat in flour and braise in fat until brown.
3. Add water, cover and heat to boiling point. Reduce heat and simmer 1 1/2 hours or until tender.
4. Add green peppers and onions after 1 hour.
5. Mix flour and water and stir until smooth. Add Worcestershire sauce, bay leaves, parsley and paprika. Heat to boiling point and boil for 2 minutes, stirring constantly.
6. Pour gravy over meat and reheat.
7. Add salt and pepper, tomatoes.
8. Mix together and simmer for 15 minutes.

99

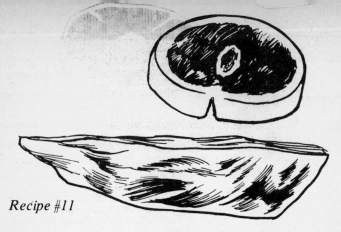

Recipe #11

VENISON LOAF
(use neck, shoulders, breast, shanks, legs or any boneless meat)

Ingredients   For 6-8 Servings

Boneless venison, ground	3 lb.
Onions, finely chopped	1/4 lb.
Celery, finely chopped	1/4 lb.
Garlic, finely chopped	1/8 clove
Bread crumbs, soft	1/4 lb.
Corn flakes	2 oz.
Salt	to taste
Pepper	to taste
Eggs	4
Meat stock	1/2 cup
Bacon fat	as directed

Step 1. Combine meat, onions, celery, and garlic.
2. Add bread crumbs, salt, pepper, slightly beaten eggs, corn flakes and stock. Mix well.
3. Mold into loaves 4 in. wide by 3 in. high. Place in baking pans. Brush tops of loaves with bacon fat.
4. Bake uncovered and without water at constant temperature in moderate oven 325 degrees F. for 1 1/2 hours or until cooked as desired. Avoid overcooking.

Note— Meat stock can be made from bouillon cubes.

Recipe #12

KIDNEY AND VENISON PIE
(use kidneys and legs, shoulders or steaks)

Ingredients   For 6-8 Servings

Kidneys	2 from your deer
Water	as directed
Boneless venison	3 lb.
Salt	to taste
Pepper	to taste
Flour, sifted	2 oz.
Fat	2 oz.
Water	1 pint
Biscuit dough	as directed

Step 1. Clean kidneys, slice into small pieces and wash under cold water. Place in container and cover with cold water. Add 1 teaspoon salt and 1 tablespoon vinegar. Soak for 20 minutes, then drain. Repeat soaking procedure. Then drain and wash. Cover with water in a tightly covered pot. Heat to boiling point, reduce heat and simmer about 45 minutes or until tender. Drain.

2. Mix salt, pepper and one half of the flour together.

3. Cut venison into 1/2 inch cubes. Roll in flour mixture. Cook in fat until brown.

4. Add water, braise in slow oven 300 degrees F. for 1 to 1 1/2 hours or until tender. Drain.

5. Mix remaining flour and small amount of cold water. Stir until smooth; add slowly to hot venison liquid. Heat to boiling point, boil 2 minutes, stirring constantly.

6. Combine kidneys, venison and gravy. Place in baking pan.

7. Use any biscuit dough, cover meat mixture with dough.

8. Bake in hot oven 425 degrees F. until brown.

Recipe #13

VENISON LEG ROAST
(use leg or rump roast only)

Ingredients   For 6-8 Servings

Venison with bone .... 6 lb.
      or
Boneless venison .... 4 lb.
Salt .... to taste
Pepper .... to taste
Garlic .... 2 small pieces

Step 1. Rub meat all around with salt and pepper. Stab
       holes in venison roast and insert pieces of garlic.
       Bake with fat side up.
  2. Roast uncovered at constant temperature in
       moderate oven 325 degrees F. for approximate-
       ly 2 hours. Turn frequently.
  3. Carve thin slices across the grain and serve
       immediately.

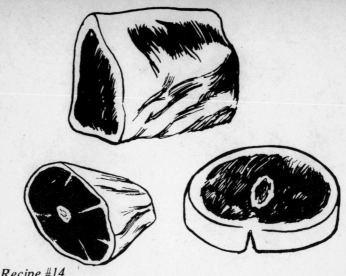

Recipe #14

BARBECUED VENISON HAMBURGERS
(use shoulders, neck, shanks or legs)

Ingredients   For 6-8 Servings

Boneless venison, chopped .... 3 lb.
Bread crumbs, seasoned .... 4 oz.
Eggs 2
Onions, chopped .... 3 small ones
Catsup .... 3 tablespoons
Worcestershire sauce .... 1/2 teaspoon
Mustard .... 1 teaspoon
Salt .... to taste
Pepper .... to taste

Step 1. Combine venison, bread crumbs, beaten eggs, chopped onions, catsup, salt and pepper.
    2. Shape into patties about 1/2 inch thick.
    3. Combine Worcestershire sauce and mustard, and brush on patties.
    4. Bake in moderate oven 350 degrees F. for 20 minutes. Top with slices of American cheese and continue baking until cheese bubbles or is slightly brown, about 10 minutes.
    5. Onion may be used instead of cheese.

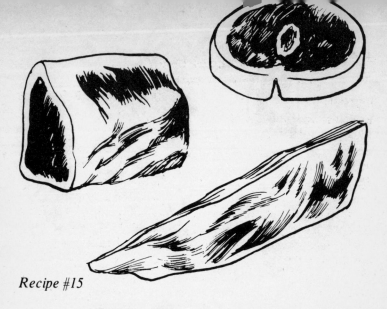

Recipe #15

VENISON MEAT BALLS WITH PORK
(use neck, shoulders, breast, shanks or legs)

Ingredients   For 6-8 Servings

Boneless venison	2 lb.
Fresh pork butt	2 lb.
Bread crumbs	1/2 lb.
Eggs	2
Onions, chopped	1/2 lb.
Salt	1 tablespoon
Pepper	to taste
Water	1/4 cup
Spaghetti sauce	as desired

Step 1. Cut venison and pork in small pieces and grind in home grinder.

     2. Saute onions until tender but not brown.

     3. Mix all ingredients together, thoroughly.

     4. Shape into 2 oz. meatballs. (Eight meatballs to a lb.)

     5. Place in greased baking pan, cook in hot oven 400 degrees F. until brown on all sides.

     6. Drop in spaghetti sauce and cook about 20 minutes. Serve hot.

104

VENISON CURRY

(use neck, shoulders, shanks, rump or legs)

Ingredients   For 6-8 Servings

Boneless venison, diced	4 lb.
Rice, uncooked	1/2 lb.
Salt	1 teaspoon
Water, boiling	1 1/2 qt.
Flour, sifted	3 oz.
Fat	1/2 pint
Milk, evaporated	1 can (14 1/2 oz.)
Water (for milk)	1/2 pint
Salt	1 tablespoon
Pepper, red	to taste
Curry powder	1 tablespoon
Cinnamon	1/4 teaspoon
Nutmeg	pinch
Cloves, ground	1/8 teaspoon
Allspice	1/8 teaspoon
Onions, chopped	1/4 lb.
Apples, sliced	1/2 lb.

Step 1. Cook venison in fat until half done, turning frequently. Remove from heat.

2. Wash rice thoroughly. Add to rapid boiling salt water. Boil 15 to 20 minutes or until tender. Drain well. This can be done at the same time you begin to cook your venison.

3. Mix flour and half of the melted fat; stir until smooth.

4. Mix milk and water; heat. Add to flour mixture. Heat to boiling point and boil for 3 minutes, stirring constantly.

5. Mix remaining fat, salt, pepper, curry powder, cinnamon, cloves, nutmeg, and allspice together.

6. Add onions, apples, and meat. Cover and heat to boiling point; reduce heat and simmer slowly for 30 minutes. Add to hot white sauce (flour mixture).

7. Reheat rice by serving curried venison over rice.

Note— If desired, rice may be started later in preparation to be served hot.

Recipe #17

DICED VENISON IN GRAVY
(use steaks, chops, cutlets or legs)

Ingredients   For 6-8 Servings

Boneless venison, diced .... 3 1/2 lb.
Onions, chopped .... 1/4 lb.
Bacon fat .... 1/4 lb.
Flour, sifted .... 2 oz.
Bouillon stock, hot .... 1 qt.
Salt .... 1 teaspoon
Milk, evaporated .... 1 can (14 1/2 oz.)
Water (for milk) .... 1 pint
Pepper .... to taste
Bread, toasted .... 2 slices per serv-
                                                              ing

Step 1. Brown diced venison in bacon fat until tender.
Do not overcook. Venison should be diced in
small pieces (1/4 in. pieces). This can be done
before or after cooking. Remove from heat.
Remove venison from frypan.

2. Make bouillon stock by using cubes and water.
Heat to boiling point, stirring constantly.

3. Cook onions slowly in fat until tender. Add flour
and mix well.

4. Add bouillon stock gradually. Heat to boiling
point, stirring constantly.

5. Mix milk and water. Add milk, salt and pepper
to hot onion mixture. Heat to boiling point. Boil
about 3 minutes, stirring constantly. Remove
from heat.

6. Add cooked venison. Reheat to serving temperature.

7. Serve over toast.

Recipe #18

VENISON CHOPS CASSEROLE
(use rib or loin chops or leg cutlets)

Ingredients   For 6-8 Servings

Venison chops .... 5 lb.
Rice .... 1/2 lb.
Green peppers, chopped .... 1/2 lb.
Onions, diced .... 1/4 lb.
Salt .... 1/2 oz.
Pepper .... 1/2 teaspoon
Tomatoes .... 1 can # 2
Water .... as needed
Fat .... as needed

Step 1. Cook rice and set aside.
    2. Brown venison chops in fat, turning frequently.
    3. Remove chops from pan, add cooked rice, and brown slightly.
    4. Combine browned rice with green peppers, onions, and seasonings.
    5. Add tomatoes.
    6. Place browned venison chops on top of rice mixture and cover. Cook in moderate oven 350 degrees F. for 1 to 1 1/2 hours, checking frequently. As rice absorbs the liquid, add more water.

107

Recipe #19

VENISON SAUERBRATEN
(use shoulders or legs)

Ingredients   For 6-8 Servings

Boneless venison .... 4 lb.
Vinegar .... 6 oz.
Water .... 3/4 cup
Onions, sliced .... 1/2 lb.
Bay leaves 3
Whole cloves 4
Salt .... 3 teaspoons
Pepper .... to taste
Fat .... 1/4 lb.
Pickling spices .... 2 tablespoons
Flour .... 2 oz.

Step 1. Place venison in bowl, add vinegar, enough water to cover meat, bay leaves, cloves, salt, pepper, onions and pickling spices; blend.
2. Let stand 24 hours before cooking.
3. Melt fat in heavy fry pan or dutch oven. Add meat and brown thoroughly on all sides.
4. Add brine in which venison was soaking. Brine should cover 1/4 of venison.
5. Cover; simmer over low heat for 3 hours or until meat is tender.
6. Remove meat, strain juices in pan. Gravy can be made by combining flour, juices, salt and pepper. Reheat, stirring constantly.
7. Venison should be sliced thin and served with hot gravy over it.

Note— This recipe must stand overnight. See Step 2.

STUFFED AND BRAISED VENISON HEART

Ingredients   For 2-3 Servings

Deer heart .... from your deer
Salt .... to taste
Pepper .... to taste
Onions, diced .... as needed
Celery, diced .... as needed
Fat .... as needed
Bread crumbs .... 2 tablespoons
Poultry seasoning .... pinch
Parsley, chopped .... pinch
Eggs, beaten 2
Bouillon, hot .... as directed

Step 1. Slice heart down center, but not in half. Wash heart in warm water and remove arteries and veins. Wash again, drain and sprinkle with salt and pepper.

2. Cook onions and celery in fat until brown. Add bread crumbs, sprinkle salt and pepper, poultry seasoning and parsley. Remove from heat.

3. Add beaten eggs and a little bouillon stock to moisten; mix lightly.

4. Fill heart with hot stuffing. Tie or secure with toothpicks.

5. Place heart in a pot that can be covered tightly. Add fat and cook until brown.

6. Add small amount of bouillon stock, cover and braise in slow oven 325 degrees F. for 2 hours or until tender. Add more bouillon during cooking if necessary.

7. Remove heart; cut into slices across the heart so that stuffing will be in center of heart.

Note— Brown gravy can be served with this recipe. Since deer hearts vary with the size of each animal, the amount of stuffing you will need will, naturally, depend on the size of the heart.

Recipe #21

SIMMERED DEER TONGUE

Ingredients   For 1-2 Servings

Deer tongue .... from your deer
Water .... 1 qt.
Onions, chopped .... 1/4 lb.
Carrots, sliced 1
Green peppers, chopped 2
Salt .... as needed
Pepper .... as needed

Step 1. Put tongue in pot and cover with water. Add all
other ingredients.

2. Cover and heat to boiling point, then reduce
heat and simmer until tongue is tender.

3. Remove tongue from broth and plunge into cold
water. Remove skin and cut away roots.

4. If tongue is to be served hot, return to cooking
water and heat to serving temperature.

Recipe #22

VENISON CUTLETS ITALIAN STYLE
(use legs or leg steaks)

Ingredients   For 6-8 Servings

Boneless venison .... 3 lb.
Fat, shortening or oil .... 1/2 lb.
Pepper .... to taste
Salt .... to taste
Eggs, beaten 3
Bread crumbs, seasoned .... 1/2 lb.
Italian cheese, grated .... 1/2 oz.

Step 1. Slice meat to portion size, as thin as possible (as
you would buy Italian veal cutlets).
   2. Put shortening or oil in frypan and heat.
   3. Add salt and pepper to beaten eggs in dish.
   4. Mix cheese and seasoned bread crumbs together
in separate dish.
   5. Dip venison in egg batter, then roll in bread
crumb mixture. Place in hot shortening or oil,
turning frequently.
   6. Remove venison when tender, approximately 20
to 30 minutes. Serve hot.

VENISON SOUP WITH VEGETABLES
(use necks, shanks or shoulders)

Ingredients	For 6-8 Servings
Venison shanks	2 from your deer
or	
Venison shoulder	3 to 4 lb.
Water	1 1/2 qt.
Pepper	to taste
Celery, diced	1/2 lb.
Onions, sliced	1/4 lb.
Turnips, sliced	1/4 lb.
Carrots, sliced	1/4 lb.
Potatoes, diced	1/2 lb.
Tomatoes	1 can # 303
Salt	1 tablespoon
Egg noodles	as desired
Garlic	1 clove
Worcestershire sauce	1 teaspoon

Step 1. Wash venison thoroughly. Cut into 2 inch cubes. Cook in water for one hour.

2. Add pepper, salt, onions, celery, turnips, carrots, garlic and tomatoes. Mix well.

3. Cover and heat to boiling point; reduce heat and simmer for approximately 1 1/2 hours.

4. Potatoes should be added about 20 minutes before cooking is completed; noodles about 10 minutes before cooking is completed.

5. Add Worcestershire sauce just before serving. Serve hot.

Recipe #24

VENISON, BARBECUED ON CHARCOAL
(use rib chops, loin chops or leg steaks)

Ingredients   For 6-8 Servings

Venison steaks or chops .... as needed
Salt .... to taste
Pepper .... to taste
Olive oil .... 2 oz.
Oregano .... pinch

Step 1. Put charcoal in barbecue and light fire one half
hour before cooking time. Mix salt, pepper, olive oil and oregano together in dish.

2. Marinate venison steaks or chops in oil mixture
for approximately 30 minutes, turning frequently.

3. Put venison on grill, turning frequently to desired cooking time; about 20 minutes for rare.

Note— Olive oil and oregano may be omitted if desired. Venison steaks may also be cooked as you would normally cook beef steaks.

113

Recipe #25

BARBECUE SAUCE FOR VENISON

Ingredients   For 6-8 Servings

Tomato puree	1 large can
Catsup	1/2 cup
Water	2 cups
Vinegar	4 tablespoons
Worcestershire sauce	1 teaspoon
Bacon, diced	1/4 lb.
Onions, diced	1/2 lb.
Brown sugar	1 tablespoon
Mustard, prepared	2 tablespoons
Salt	to taste
Pepper	to taste

In heavy saucepan, combine all ingredients;
bring to a boil. Reduce heat and simmer until
sauce thickens.

Note— Saucy venison can be made by baking or broil-
ing three to four pounds of venison, cut into
serving pieces, until it is half done and then
adding it to the warm sauce to simmer for an
hour. Served over boiled rice, this recipe will
serve six to eight people.

The sauce may also be used for other venison
recipes, or for beef or pork.

SCALE OF WEIGHTS AND MEASURES

Simplified Measurements

2 ounces = 1/8 lb.

4 ounces = 1/4 lb.

6 ounces = 3/8 lb.

8 ounces = 1/2 lb.

10 ounces = 5/8 lb.

12 ounces = 3/4 lb.

14 ounces = 7/8 lb.

16 ounces = 1 lb.

3 teaspoons = 1 tablespoon

4 tablespoons = 1/4 cup

5 1/3 tablespoons = 1/3 cup

8 tablespoons = 1/2 cup

12 tablespoons = 2/3 cup

16 tablespoons = 1 cup

1 cup = 1/2 pint

2 cups = 1 pint

2 pints (4 cups) = 1 quart

4 quarts = 1 gallon

The above scale of weights and measures should help to make the recipes in this book easier for you to understand. Also, most of the recipes in this book have been written to serve six to eight people. In the event that this is too much for your family, the recipes can be easily altered to suit your own needs.

Any vegetable such as mashed potatoes, French fries, peas and carrots, corn, asparagus and broccoli can be served with venison. If desired, wild plum jelly can be used with venison, while mint jelly goes well on young does and fawn.

GLOSSARY

Aging a Deer—Determining the age of a deer.

Aging Meat—Hanging deer for a certain period of time at certain temperatures to help bring out the full flavor of the meat.

'At-the-ready'—Hunter alert and prepared to fire his rifle.

Browsing Area—Area where deer feed.

Buck—Male deer.

Camouflage—Apparel and equipment of such a color and form as to blend with the natural foliage or environment.

Doe—Female deer.

Doe Day—A day determined by the authorities when, in addition to a buck, a doe may be considered a suitable target.

Drivers—The active members of the drive.

Driving—Actively moving forward to rouse deer from area of the hunt, i.e. to get the deer on the move.

Fawn—Young deer of either sex with spots still on skin. Spots usually disappear at approximately four months of age.

Field-dress—To "gut" or eviscerate a deer in the field soon after it has been killed.

Flag—The white tail of the deer. When the tail drops (the flag is down) the deer is usually in distress.

Gaminess—Poor taste of meat due to poor field-dressing or improper aging procedure.

N.R.A.—National Rifle Association

A national organization concerned with promoting interest and training in the safe and proper utilization of the rifle. It has been the first line of defense in the rights of the individual to own and use his rifle legally.

Party Permit—A special license granted by the state to two or more hunters to shoot an extra deer of either sex.

Point—A single projection at least one inch long on each antler.

Posted land—Privately owned land on which hunting is forbidden except by special permission.

Posting—Standing or sitting in one position waiting for deer to come into your zone of fire.

Rack—Antlers or horns that sprout from the head of deer.

Scope—Shortened form of telescopic sight.

Sling—Leather strap on rifle extending from barrel to stock. Used to help carry rifle over shoulder.

Spike buck—Male deer with two horns, each horn three inches in length or over.

"Spook"—To arouse or alert deer to the point that he will move.

Stand—A site, constructed eight or twelve feet high in a tree, from which the hunter observes and shoots his deer.

Tag a Deer—Attaching a part of the license to the recently killed deer.

Velvet—Thickened covering over the antlers. Latest opinion is that it is a heavy concentration of blood vessels that aid in the radiation of body heat.

Vent—Opening at base of tail through which solid wastes are excreted.

THE END OF A SUCCESSFUL HUNT